Kermit

MW00677773

748.4

The Christian Adventure

THE CHRISTIAN ADVENTURE

Edward E. Thornton

BROADMAN PRESS
NASHVILLE, TENNESSEE

© Copyright 1991 ● Broadman Press
All rights reserved
4254-50
ISBN: 0-8054-5450-0
Dewey Decimal Classification: 253.5
Subject Heading: MINISTERS // COUNSELING
Library of Congress Catalog Card Number: 90-45647
Printed in the United States of America

Unless otherwise indicated, Scripture is from the *New Revised Standard Version Bible* copyright © 1989, by the Division of Christian Education of the National Council of Churches of Christ in the United States of America, and used by permission. References marked KJV are from the *King James Version.* References marked GNB are from the *Good News Bible,* the Bible in Today's English Version. Old Testament: Copyright © American Bible Society 1976; New Testament: Copyright © American Bible Society 1966, 1971, 1976. Used by permission. Scripture in a "A Day at the Lake" (chapter 4) is quoted or modified from *The Cotton Patch Version of Matthew and John*, and *The Cotton Patch Version of Luke and Acts,* © copyright Association Press 1970, 1969, and used by permission.

Library of Congress Cataloging-in-Publication Data
Thornton, Edward E.
    The Christian Adventure / Edward E. Thornton.
      p.   cm.   — (The Bible and personal crisis)
    Includes bibliographical references.
    ISBN 0-8054-5450-0
    1. Desire for God. 2. Spiritual life—Baptist authors.
3. Pastoral counseling.   I. Title.   II. Series.
BV4817.T48 1991
248.4—dc20
                                               90-45647
                                                  CIP

To
Bani Shorter
Analyst and Spiritual Guide
who enabled me
to recover my story
and
to reclaim THE Story

Contents

The Christian Adventure

Introduction

The story of Jesus invites you into an adventure in living that is remarkably exciting and fulfilling. The story serves as a guide for the adventure as well. The adventure of living the Jesus life has little in common with carnival rides or athletic contests where you can enter the ride or contest, know the limits and rules in advance, and walk away at a given time, returning to the safe boundaries of ordinary living again. Living the Jesus life begins in a wilderness, leads to the death of your sense of self-importance, and in the end leaves your old self behind—an empty tomb. It is a life of constant conflict and profound joy. It zigzags between surprise and mystery, absolute slavery and radical freedom.

The Bible and Personal Crisis

The "crisis" to which this volume speaks is not one of the many problems of life. It is, rather, *the* problem of life. To put it another way, everyone must deal with "problems of living," and for these problems specific guidance can be given based on current research in pastoral care and counseling. Underlying the "problems of living," however, is the "predicament" of being human. The human predicament consists of our vulnerability to disease, disaster, and death; our limitations of perception, problem solving, and powerlessness; the biologically based contradictions in the structure of our brains and in patterns of sexual response; the social complications ingrained in sex roles, authority patterns, and ethnic traditions; and ultimately, the

fragmentary and competing values by which we try to make
meaning out of life. The human "predicament" compounds every one of the "problems of living." Even when relatively problem free, we may have restless nights and anxious days, dimly
aware of the inexorable "predicament" of being human.

It is to the dis-ease of our "predicament" as human beings
that the Bible speaks most clearly and profoundly. Nowhere is
the message clearer than in the life of Jesus as recorded in the
four Gospels. In the Jesus way of life we both hear and see a way
of coping with the human "predicament." The more aware we
become, the more we see through the surface features of Jesus'
life in the context of first-century Judaism. We are moved by a
wisdom that infuses all races, cultures, and times. We sense in
the Jesus' life a way of welcoming our "predicament," experiencing the presence of God in our "predicament," and making
meaning in the company of those with whom we share the Way.

No wonder, then, that the Christian adventure appeals
strongly to people who are not in the mainstream and those
who are in a life-style crisis. Jesus faced criticism for making
friends with people who were on the margins of society. He re-
minded His critics, "Those who are well have no need of a phy-
sician, but those who are sick; I have come to call not the right-
eous but sinners to repentance" (Luke 5:31-32). Our awareness
of Jesus' bent toward people in pain and in crisis, people excluded and oppressed, has shaped this entire collection of books on
"The Bible and Personal Crisis." We wanted, therefore, to de-
vote this final volume to an original retelling of the Jesus story.
The Christian adventure in living the Jesus life is the most
down-to-earth response of the Bible to our perpetual crisis—the
human "predicament."

The prior volumes in "The Bible and Personal Crisis" collection have guided readers through underground realms of fear,
loneliness, and self-defeating life-styles into the freedom of the
fear (reverence) of God, companionship of the Spirit, and self-
surrender. They have challenged readers to look at the pitfalls
in marriage and find secure footing in marital relationships for

the journey through every stage of family life. Guidance at the crossroads of personal spiritual growth is balanced with realistic and wise counsel for the gathered people of God about the power of the church to help and to hurt.

The possibilities for newness of life in the midst of the traumas of a shattered vocation and the confusion of living in codependent relationships bring good news to people in crises, but only recently have these themes received attention. Guidelines for talking so teenagers will listen also blend biblical principles with practical help. In the context of these practical and often-frightening concerns, this final volume reaches toward the ultimate hope in *The Christian Adventure.*

Stories: Your Story, My Stories, and the Jesus Story

The great adventure for a Christian is creating a little story with one's own life that fits into the epic story of Jesus, the Christ of human history. My greatest challenge in writing *The Christian Adventure* was to find words and stories to awaken (or reawaken) in you the awareness that your life is potentially a chapter in the ongoing Jesus story.

You and I want energy that will empower us to weave all the broken pieces of life into a pattern that harmonizes with Jesus' life. The only energy I know that can do this is the energy that flows out of God's love for you and your responding desire for God. Your persistent and sometimes passionate desire for God will enable you to find your reason for being; it will sustain you on the adventure of living.

The desire for God enslaves, and yet in so doing sets you free. Everyone may be described as packaged desire. The package of being human includes desire for safety and for survival, for self-esteem and for belonging, for power and for love. It combines desire for adventure and for being at home, for change and for the familiar, for oneness with all that is, and for unique creativity. With desire you hate, and with desire you love. With desire you destroy, and with desire you create. With desire you stretch and grow, and with desire you shrink back and get stuck. *Desire* is the combustion engine in your attachments. *Will* is sitting in the driver's seat. When both *desire* and *will* are driven by and centered on perfect love, you are then both slave of God and totally free.

The Christian Adventure lifts the veil of repression that can prevent you from experiencing your desire for God. Sometimes repression of a passionate love for God is maintained by being overly familiar with the Jesus story. Simply hearing the story over and over again may lead you to believe that you know it and that in knowing it, you are living it fully. My first task, therefore, is to retell the story in an original way that will help you see it for the first time. The stories I have written for each chapter are based on solid historical facts. I stand within the biblical accounts and view the gospel stories through the eyes of biblical characters in the main. Active imagination takes over then in creating the story. The result is historical fiction. The outcome, I hope, is that some facets of the Jesus story previously missed will sparkle, catch your eye, and give you insight in the retelling of it in fictional form.

Next, I want to encourage you to trust the subtle stirrings of your desire. I shall try to cultivate and nourish your longings for the inner freedom that is the harvest of living the Jesus life. Toward this end, I shall offer comments on the short stories I have written and elaborate on the stories' themes to amplify the Jesus story.

I would like for you to discover that the desire for God, unlike all other human desires, is nonaddictive. The more you feed desire for God in living the Jesus story the more freedom you have from the desires that tend to constrict the spirit, bind the mind, choke compassion, consume and waste energy, and shrivel the soul.

The core of *The Christian Adventure* is, then, a book of short stories about the Jesus story. Marker events in the life of Jesus are retold in original ways, as though seen through the eyes of people who came within His circle. Comments on the action, the characters, and the themes of these stories yield a rich harvest. These comments point up the need for a spirituality that sees God at work changing the religious and political structures of society as well as renewing individuals. They capture the agonizing conflict between belief and unbelief, the human struggle to trust the evidence of God's presence in the everyday world. They prepare you for the requirements of costly discipleship.

Some of the dangers of living the Jesus life are noted, as well, such as giving yourself to the cruelty born of a lust for power in the name of God and becoming unaware of the hardening of your heart against the power of love. Making a big deal of spirituality limits your ability to see the sacred in the everyday; it can seduce you into wearing the mask of self-righteousness.

Surprises about the spiritual life spring up at every turn. Given Jesus' claim to be one with God, for example, Jesus' death means that God was crucified as a common criminal. Such a thought was foolishness to the Greeks and madness to the Jews. This was the parting of the ways for the people of Jesus' day. The call to take up a cross and follow Jesus forces the same choice for the person who is seeking to find inner freedom and spiritual power in society today. Herein is the dark mystery of discipleship, the core of Christian spirituality, and the central theme of the Jesus story.

Part of the wonder and beauty of stories is the way they can tune a person to the experience of those who have no conscious desire for God at all, those whose desire is frustrated by the absence of God, and those whose desire for God is nourished by the Presence who responds to and feeds their desire with delight. These stories help make sense out of life, no matter where you are at this point. At the same time these stories help to empower you to live out your desire for God without falling into despair or self-deception.

Behind the Stories

Behind the stories are the questions that kept haunting and driving me as this book was being formed. Foremost was the question: How can I draw the reader into the world of Jesus and into Jesus' mind and heart, not just into the external features of that world? Soon another question reared its head: How can I be fair in developing an appreciation of all of the characters of the story? For instance, according to ancient tradition, both Pilate and his wife, Claudia, became Christians some years after the crucifixion of Jesus. Pilate was declared a saint by the Coptic Church and Claudia by the Greek Orthodox Church in subsequent centuries. So how can I develop their characters in such a way that the reader will sense both the shamefulness of Pilate's bondage to his own career and his potential for radical transformation?

Every event has not only the "good characters" and the "bad characters" but also the "little ones"; those who are unnamed and unsung. How can the "little ones" who are so significant in the Jesus story be given faces? Can they become objects of identification for all of us—we who are the nameless "little ones" in the Jesus story being written in our generation?

Always one concern kept recurring like the images in a kaleidoscope: How can I prepare the way for the openings of the reader's heart to the Holy Spirit? How quicken hope in the Jesus story to become a source of spiritual growth today? How inspire and empower for the Christian adventure? How leave you with a clearer vision of your destination, a greater delight in yourself as an adventurer on your own pilgrimage, and as the author who is writing your chapter in the epic story of Jesus? Also, how can I leave you with deeper confidence in the ultimate success of the adventure to which you have committed your life?

Alongside of these driving questions lies the actual work of authorship. A decade of active searching, enjoying, and being formed by the master stories of the ages gave me confidence for the task. Years of tracing out with students the stages of the spiritual journey and the dynamics of religious experience in the masterpieces of Christian "pilgrimage" literature have whetted my appetite more and more to return to the source of the Christian pilgrimage, the Jesus story. Dante's *The Divine Comedy,* Bunyan's *Pilgrim's Progress,* and Tolkien's *The Lord of the Rings* mark off the epochs of "pilgrimage" stories from the high Middle Ages to the twentieth century. Permeating them all is the simple story of Jesus, told in four versions: Mark, Luke, Matthew, and John.

For the better part of two years now, I have reexplored the four Gospels.[1] Immersion in Jesus' world and Jesus' own mind and spirit has drawn me deeper and deeper into history. For example, how can one understand the mind of Jesus without paying attention to Jesus' Scripture (which we call the Old Testament)? I gave particular attention to the Torah (the first five books of the Old Testament) and the prophets.[2] After all, on the mount of transfiguration it was Moses and Elijah who appeared with Jesus: embodiments of the Law and the Prophets. Worship, too, was central in Jesus' formation. So the Jerusalem temple became a focus of study, and, of course, the synagogues.[3]

Jesus' life was formed by the structures of the family and kinship groups, and by social mores, as well as by the Scriptures;[4] by political and economic systems, as well as by religious institutions; by the heroes and the villains of His day and times.[5] This called for familiarity with the Greek and Roman worlds, with Egypt and the mystery religions, as the major world powers and cultural forces within which Israel was wrapped, by which she was ruled, oppressed, and ultimately destroyed and dispersed throughout the Mediterranean world.[6] In every area of study, I held to the goal of understanding the cutting edge of biblical studies. Excellent consultation guided me and also held my feet to the fire of this standard of knowledge.

Writing my stories about the Jesus story required more than a warehouse full of information about the life and times of Jesus. The task called for me to hone the skills of writing fiction as well.[7]

Finally, and most crucial for accomplishing my purpose in *The Christian Adventure,* I had to risk taking my own adventure in imagination. At this point, I became most vulnerable to the

Jesus story. Imagination meant actively seeking and listening to the subtle sounds and gentle promptings of the Holy Spirit within. Every marker event in the life of Jesus offers many characters through whom to view and tell the story, many complications that might be developed in the action, and multiple themes worthy of treatment. The discipline to which I gave myself was simply to "ask, . . . search, . . . knock," trusting the "heavenly Father [to] give the Holy Spirit" for guidance (Luke 11:9-13).

My sense of the finished work is that I have brought a vial of perfume (purchased with the equivalent of a full year's pay) and broken it over the world-weary feet of Jesus. In other words, the writing of *The Christian Adventure has been an act of devotion. In doing so, I am fulfilled. I only hope some of the aroma comes through these pages to you.*

Notes

1. See bibliography for recommended introductions to the Gospels as story.

2. See bibliography for a list of commentaries and Bible dictionaries used most consistently.

3. Andre Parrot, *The Temple of Jerusalem* (London: SCM, 1957).

4. For sources on daily life in the time of Jesus, see bibliography.

5. See bibliography for sources on the political movements in Jesus' day.

6. See bibliography for sources on the religions of the Greek and Roman worlds.

7. See bibliography for sources used to write fiction.

1

A People Prepared

Where does the Jesus story begin? In the Gospel according to Mark it begins with the preaching of John the Baptist, preparing the way for Israel to welcome Jesus as their promised Messiah. Luke's Gospel, the next to be written, begins earlier in time. Luke begins with the annunciation of the angel, Gabriel, to Zechariah, the father of John the Baptist, and then continues to tell of the annunciations to Mary and to Joseph of the coming birth of Jesus. Matthew, written about the time of Luke but somewhat later, begins with the genealogy of Jesus Christ, starting with Abraham. The Fourth Gospel opens with the words, "In the beginning was the Word, and the Word was with God, and the Word was God. He was in the beginning with God. All things came into being through him, and without him not one thing came into being" (John 1:1-3).

Each new version of the Jesus story pushed the beginning back: first the preaching of John the Baptist; then the announcement of John's conception and birth; then to Abraham, the father of the Jews; and finally into eternity, in the creation, and in the mind of God. The pattern becomes increasingly clear as the Gospel stories were written: the Jesus story begins in the purposes of God to make ready a people prepared. Jesus' coming is central to the great design of creation. It is anticipated in Abraham with the inception of Israel. Announcement is made to the parents of John and of Jesus. Thirty years later John the Baptist announced the coming of Jesus to the nation.

Could it be that the story of the whole human race is written in the great design of creation? Is it possible that world events as well as individual lives are shaped by the spiritual awareness of the "people prepared"? The visions that are received, the prayers that are prayed, the communities that preserve and proclaim the vision, and the faithfulness of the nameless ones in out-of-the-way places of the earth—do these acts actually serve the purposes of the divine within a master plan? Questions such as these began to occur to the early Christians as they reflected on the Jesus story.

To enter into the mind of some of those closest to the events at the coming of Jesus, join me now in imagination as a reporter interviews Zechariah to gather data for a story for the *Jerusalem Sabbath Magazine.* Zechariah, the father of John the Baptist, is near the end of his life, now in his late eighties. The reporter failed to leave behind a copy of his questions, so we will have to imagine what was asked. The following pages contain the responses Zechariah gave to the reporter's questions.

Story: The Miracle Mothers

[INTERVIEWER]

ZECHARIAH: So you came to old man Zechariah for a slant on the story about the boys—our John and Cousin Jesus?

You know, I'm not in the Messiah movement anymore, myself. 'Course Lizzie was. Right up to the day she died, in her eighty-eighth year. It was for her that I stayed on the rolls. After her death I dropped out. Really, though, as far as the movement goes, I gave up on it after they murdered the boys. When they sent home the corpse of our boy John for us to bury . . . ! Then they betrayed the faith, double-crossed our nation in dealing with Pilate, and got Jesus nailed to a Roman cross. That's when I gave up on politics.

[INTERVIEWER]

ZECHARIAH: No! Don't get me wrong! I did not say that God was not in the movement. What I said was, I gave up on the politics. Truth is, Cousin Jesus gave up on the politics first. Lizzie never agreed with Jesus deciding to go for "a spiritual kingdom." She would pound the table with her tiny fist and plead, "Jesus, please listen to common sense!" We could all see what was coming. The party leaders were all getting in line behind old Caiaphas, the high priest, to do Jesus in.

Now John, our boy, was a smart politician. He went to the people, stayed away from the temple crowd, kept moving, too, so that not even Rome knew where he was most of the time. Lizzie was in the thick of it in those days. She always said, "Zach, you would have been high priest today, and John would be one of your chief priests, if Cousin Jesus had had the guts to step up and lead the movement that we had going."

[INTERVIEWER]

ZECHARIAH: Well, that was just Lizzie. She called it like she saw it. Yes, she was an activist—and more. She was probably the best strategist the boys had in the movement. Tough, too. Thin, wiry little thing. A ball of fire all the time.

[INTERVIEWER]

ZECHARIAH: Indeed there were some "strange happenings" as you put it, around the birth of our boy, John. I had incense duty at the temple one high holy day. We had a huge crowd: "Heads on toes during prayers," we priests used to say. I can see it as plain as if it were this morning. I had to pass through the curtain of golden chains into the holy place alone, censing as I went. The incense just hung in the space, seeming not to rise to those latticed windows at the roof. Then just as I placed the censer on the altar, standing at the right side of the altar of incense, he appeared. He was more real than you are to me right now. He was standing there—aflame, dancing with energy; every particle of smoke in the holy place a golden spark. I was embraced by his presence. He spoke to me and gave me his name: "I am Gabriel. I stand in the presence of God, and I have been sent to speak to you and to bring you this good news."

He said that Elizabeth and I would have a son, and we would name him John. I saw his life unfold before my eyes. He would take the vow of the Nazirites for life. He would be a radical reformer, a second Elijah. Gabriel's words ring in my ears to this day: our boy was "*to make ready for the Lord a people prepared.*"

As I imagined my son as a leader of the people, fear gripped me. Fear of being ripped out of my safe and comfortable priesthood. Fear of our becoming a political family—what Lizzie had always wanted us to be. Most of all, fear my imagination was running amok. I began to reason and to doubt. Lizzie was already past her menopause. As a priest, I knew that visions could trick the mind. (We priests are always having to evaluate these reports, you know.) I could be put out to pasture myself if I believed what was happening to me in that moment. Such things just must never happen in the temple, of all places.

How could I deny the reality of the vision? And then Gabriel spoke again: "Because you did not believe my words, which will be fulfilled in their time, you will become mute, unable to speak, until the day these things occur" (Luke 1:19-20). How I needed to be mute that following year! There was so much commotion in the priesthood . . . inquiries . . . allegations . . . threats of disciplinary actions . . . radicals invading the temple grounds with their placards and chants . . . our entire temple staff put on probation by the office of the Roman procurator.

[INTERVIEWER]

ZECHARIAH: Do I believe that God was in it? Listen, my young reporter, I do not *believe* that God was in it—I *KNOW* God was in it. I know who met me at the altar of incense. It is not a matter for believing. It is a *certitude*. In those days heaven was a flurry of activity getting ready for the birth of these two boys: "[*making*] *ready a people prepared for the Lord.*"

[INTERVIEWER]

ZECHARIAH: You had not heard about the appearance to Mary? Well, I'm surprised they aren't talking about it in the movement. Mary is a very private person, though, as you will see when you interview her for your story.

Yes, the angel Gabriel came to Mary right after she and

Joseph were betrothed. He told her she would bear a son and
should name Him Jesus. Now, mind you, Mary and Joseph had
not consummated their marriage yet. Yes, before they came together, Mary found herself pregnant. Well, the angel also told
her about Lizzie being pregnant and in her sixth month—hit it
right on the mark. Lizzie had withdrawn from everyone for five
whole months after she knew about herself. Just as she was beginning to adjust to being pregnant, Mary came to us with her
news.

[INTERVIEWER]

ZECHARIAH: That's right. Mary made a beeline from Nazareth to our place, here in this Jerusalem suburb, as soon as she
was sure. She took it as a word from the Lord that Lizzie was to
be her substitute mother during her ordeal.

[INTERVIEWER]

ZECHARIAH: Ordeal it was. Don't you get the picture? Mary
was a young teen, betrothed to a respectable tradesman of the
house of David, and she turned up pregnant.

[INTERVIEWER]

ZECHARIAH: No, Joseph is *not* the father. When Mary
arrived at our door, she was a basket case. Joseph had made up
his mind to divorce her. Mind you it could have been worse. He
could have had her stoned to death, you know. Joseph was a
decent sort, though, and he sent her word that he would break
the contract on the Q.T., so as not to put her to shame, but he
was getting out.

[INTERVIEWER]

ZECHARIAH: Well, the angel Gabriel saved the day. You can
check this out with Mary if you want, but I have it straight from
Joseph, himself. He had a dream that told him not to be afraid
to keep Mary because she had conceived of the Holy Spirit.
That's what the dream said: Mary conceived "of the Holy
Spirit." What's more, they would have a boy and were to name
Him Jesus, because He would "save his people from their sins."

One more thing I want you to know and spread to the world.
I was with Joseph in his final illness. By that time we were dear

friends, you see. Joseph whispered to me at the last, "Zach, I never touched her until after the baby was born." I don't know to this day how Joseph had it figured, but I am certain he wanted people to know—so they could believe Mary's story.

[INTERVIEWER]

ZECHARIAH: What is Mary's side of the story? All I can tell you is what happened the three months she was with us. Most of that is from Lizzie, you understand.

First thing you've got to realize is that we are going to be talking about miracles. The miracle that just blew me away was the change that came over Lizzie from the first day that Mary walked into this house. Lizzie was barren right up until she was through menopause. She was a high-energy political activist all our married life. She left the religion stuff up to me: "That's your job," she used to say, whenever I tried to talk with her about my spiritual experiences.

Well, I was home helping get things ready when Mary arrived. I couldn't speak, you remember, so I stayed in the background most of the time. Mary no more than said, "Hello, Aunt Elizabeth," before Lizzie burst out in a voice like a person possessed, a sort of singing like. The words are carved into my mind: "Blessed are you among women, and blessed is the fruit of your womb. And why has this happened to me, that the mother of my Lord comes to me?" (Luke 1:42-43). I tell you it was as if I were back in the holy place, standing before the altar of incense, receiving the angel's words again. Lizzie was ecstatic. She was uttering inspired words: "the mother of my Lord." Lizzie was old enough to be Mary's grandmother, and she called Mary the "mother of my Lord."

From that very moment, Lizzie began to change. For the first time ever, she began to be at peace with herself—like at home in her own body, gentle with herself and with everyone around her. *Aware,* that's it. She began to be aware—aware of Mary and of me, and not just her "causes," aware of the blossoms on the almond tree.

I remember hearing her say to Mary one morning, "Mary,

notice the almond tree today. It is awakening from the sleep of
winter." And Mary responded in her bright and thoughtful
way, "So that is why we call it the 'awake tree.' It is the first tree
to awake in the springtime. Aunt Elizabeth, maybe we are like
the 'awake tree'; for we have been chosen to be the first to awak-
en to the blossoming of the Lord's presence in our land."

It was happening to both of them together. They were awakening: aware of a Presence from beyond the everyday world of
household duties and politics. It was like they knew deep down
that God was doing something in the world beyond anything
they could control, and they were both a part of it. Something
more! Lizzie let go of a curse she had carried her whole life—the
curse we priests put on every woman who is barren. She fought
her pregnancy for six months. Then, when Mary entered the
house, Lizzie was at peace with herself, with the whole world,
and most of all with the God who was making it all happen. It
was a miracle. She, Lizzie, became a whole woman. She had
found her Lord in Mary's womb. Not in the men who run the
world or plot revolutions, but in Mary's womb.

[INTERVIEWER]

ZECHARIAH: About Mary? Oh, yes, Mary was changing too,
but in the opposite direction from Lizzie. Lizzie changed from
an angry activist to a relaxed, compassionate woman—at peace
within herself. Stronger than ever, she was finding strength
within herself, rather than attaching herself to some would-be
prophet and being driven by hatred for her lot in life. Mary was
as different as day from night. She was a sweet one—plucked
from the meadows of Galilee. She was thoughtful but unaware
of the tensions that were tearing our country apart. She was a
child of nature—alive to the voice of the flowers and the trees,
in tune with the wind, singing the music of the spheres.

During her three months here with Lizzie, Mary changed
too. She changed from a girl to the woman who would mother a
child, from an innocent in the ways of the world to a person
wise to the evil in the social and political systems that center
here in Jerusalem. Lizzie must have told her a hundred times:

"Mary, my dear, you've got to be *wise* as serpents and harmless as doves." Mary learned her lessons well. She finally joined the Messiah movement after Jesus was crucified, and today she is a virtual "saint" to the disciples.

[INTERVIEWER]

ZECHARIAH: By the time Mary left us and went back to Galilee, her vision was at least as large as all Israel. Sometimes I wonder if she was not ahead of us all in seeing that the whole human race was about to receive the gift of God that she carried within her womb. When I think about the way Mary grew wise in the ways of the world, I say we're looking at another miracle.

[INTERVIEWER]

ZECHARIAH: About me? There's not much to tell. I stayed on here in temple service while Lizzie joined the movement. They made me an emeritus priest, you know. I do a lot of remembering now; and I wonder a lot too. Mostly, I wonder if Lizzie was right after all: Should the boys have gone for a political kingdom first and then brought in the spiritual part? God was in it all so clearly! Why, then, has it come to this? Nothing left but a young reporter doing a story for the *Jerusalem Sabbath Magazine.*

[INTERVIEWER]

ZECHARIAH: You are quite welcome. I have been pleased to help you get the story out to the public as it really was. By the way, if I were writing this story, I would entitle it, "The Miracle Mothers: Making Ready for the Lord a People Prepared."

Comments on Story: The Miracle Mothers

The action in "The Miracle Mothers" takes place at two levels. Up front we see Zechariah and Elizabeth ("Lizzie"), Mary and Joseph. They are very much a part of the everyday world. Backstage, but always present during the story, are Gabriel and God. They intrude into the see-touch world in ways that prompt Zechariah to say to the reporter, "In those days heaven was a flurry of activity." Action is intense in both worlds, the seen and the unseen, earth and heaven.

At the intersection of these two worlds, we see collision after collision. Gabriel collides with Zechariah at the altar of incense in the temple. Gabriel again crashes into the innocence of Mary, a young teen, "plucked from the meadows of Galilee." An unnamed angel of the Lord invades Joseph's sleep with a dream that lures him into a whirlpool of crises and fame he would never have asked for. Why? Because heaven had business with earth. At heaven's headquarters Gabriel was given the job of making "ready for the Lord a people prepared."

Gabriel, acting on orders from God, set up a crisis of faith for everyone who hears this story. The crisis of faith happens on two levels also. First, you are forced to decide whether to believe or doubt the reality of the presence of God there and then—in the events of the story. Second, you must decide whether to be open or closed to the presence of God here and now—acting in a similar way in you, your family, and in your world of friends and of work.

If God could break through the barrier between the seen and the unseen there and then to make ready "a people prepared" to welcome God's Self into their world, God can penetrate the barrier again and again, here and now, in you and in me, to make us ready for God as well. We must make the kind of choices the characters in the story made. Like Lizzie, we may fight the unexpected (and uninvited) new being within. She fought her new destiny for five months just as she had fought against her inmost self for a lifetime. Like Lizzie, we may be willing to be surprised by joy in discovering the presence of our Lord—just an embrace away, within our own house. Lizzie's discovery freed her from an addictive life-style as a harsh and driven person, but only because she was willing to give herself to the mystery of the presence of the Lord in the womb of her niece.

Like Mary, we may risk accepting a calling that draws us out of ourselves, out of innocence and naivete about the turmoil and evil of the world we live in. Joseph, too, was a risk taker. Or, like Zechariah, we may choose to retreat into the familiar and safe places of our old ways of life, content with a single moment of ecstasy, wondering about the possible futility of it all.

Desire for God

When we ask, "Where is the desire for God in this story?" we are in for a surprise. Initially, the four main characters have very little desire for God beyond their normal piety. Lizzie longs passionately for the coming of the Messiah, but Lizzie's messiah is a nationalistic god, not the God above gods. Zechariah serves the temple god of law and order. Not until after Gabriel's confrontation does Zechariah begin to see beyond the vindication of Israel and to hope for the "knowledge of salvation . . . the forgiveness of . . . sins [and] the tender mercy of our God" (Luke 1:77-78). Mary and Joseph both give evidence of personal piety, a respect for God, and a willingness to surrender to divine guidance. They are not captive to the political ambitions of their Jerusalem kinspeople, but neither do they give evidence of seeing beyond the boundaries of their everyday lives.

The angelic messengers of God are the ones who inject the "desire for God" into the story. The desire they inspire rises out of hope—the certain knowledge that God is acting on the stage of history. Nothing can ever be the same for these four people after God breaks through into their awareness and awakens in them the longing for God's kingdom to come "on earth as it is in heaven."

As the Jesus story opens, therefore, the desire for God is in God's desire for the people. It is up to God to awaken desire for God, and God is equal to the task. God's messengers awaken desire for God in each of the characters of the story, expand their vision of God's kingdom, and do so without compromising their freedom to accept or to reject their role in the drama.

The spotlight of the drama is not on the private lives of its four central characters, however. Their inner struggles fade out in the light of the drama of a new creation. God is working in the world to create a new community, "a people prepared" to welcome the birth of Jesus with wholehearted hospitality in their hearts, and to remember, and share the story throughout all time to come.

Events on the stage of nations and empires are being shaped by the divine interventions of the story. One thinks of such moments in modern history: when Ghandi stepped onto the stage of the British Empire and wrestled India free without firing a shot; and when the Reverend Martin Luther King, Jr., organized a bus boycott in Montgomery, Alabama, and found himself on the stage of American history, a modern Moses saying, "Let my people go!"

Stories from Today

Evidence from the 1980s suggests that God continues to be active making "ready a people prepared." Behind the crumbling of the Berlin Wall in late 1989 are two stories of Christians being transformed in their personal lives while creating the conditions for a relatively peaceful democracy revolution in Eastern Europe. Both stories took place in countries under the political domination of a Communist party. One story comes from Yugoslavia, in a village of four hundred people. The place is as obscure and insignificant as could be found in Eastern Europe. Everyone in the village belongs to the Roman Catholic parish. The second story comes from East Germany where it was played out chiefly in large, industrial cities. It has to do with the efforts of both Protestant and Roman Catholic churches to conduct ecumenical worship services without violating dictatorial laws against public demonstrations and political gatherings.

Both of these stories are about miracles. Neither of them have received as much attention in the media as they deserve. They are almost too incredible to report in the secular press or television news. Not many people are willing to risk the scorn of the secular world by reporting religious events that cannot be explained away in psychological or sociological terms. Not many religious people are willing to risk becoming objects of the hatred of other religious people whose prejudices are challenged by such events. It may be as true today as it was in Jesus' day that for God to enter human history in miraculous ways is to become a source of scandal and a stumbling stone to some secular and religious people alike. What the two stories have in common is an outpouring of religious experience among Christians. We do well to reserve judgment until all of the information is in hand and then to open our hearts to the possibility that God's ways may be beyond our ways.

The apparition of Mary.—Suppose the evening TV news was to report a story from Sweetwater, Texas. Six young people riding the fences of their adjoining ranches saw an apparition of Jesus. Jesus was beckoning to them to listen to Him. He told them that He would meet them daily in times of prayer to give them a message for the world. Night after night the TV news would then show brief clips of these young people going to their local Baptist church and coming out to tell people that Jesus is calling the world to return to the ways of God, to convert their lives to peace with God and with their fellow humans, and to pray for peace.

What would you make of such a TV news story? Imagine, as the weeks went by, that the TV news showed a team of psychologists and psychiatrists testing the young people and finding them to be normal in every way. Suppose, then, that people began to make pilgrimages to Sweetwater, Texas, that the citizens of Sweetwater decided to believe the young people, and to take it as their calling from God to be hospitable to the pilgrims and to allow their town to become a place of prayer for the world.

Then imagine that within less than ten years some twenty million people had made pilgrimages to Sweetwater, Texas, and nearly all of them had been impressed with the absence of commercialism, the spirit of prayer in the town, and their own rediscovery of faith in God and hope for the world. The TV news would be showing all the churches filled to capacity with services throughout every day of the week. Interviews with people who had come from every continent of the world would show people saying, "This town is the closest thing there is to a perfect community of love and adherence to the ways of God."

Would you want to visit Sweetwater too? Would you be open to the possibility that God had broken into the world in such a way as this to save the world from self-destruction?

Then, suppose that all of this had happened since June 24, 1981. In December, 1989, when the Berlin Wall began to crumble and an almost bloodless democracy revolution broke out in Central Europe, when the leader of Communist Russia became one of the foremost champions of peace in the world, would you wonder if the prayers of the millions of pilgrims to Sweetwater, Texas, were being answered on the stage of world history?

Of course this did not happen in Sweetwater, Texas. But some believe it did happen in a similar way in the village of Medjugorje (pronounced: med-ju-gor-e), Yugoslavia, a Roman Catholic village of about four hundred people. A group of young people reported that they saw an apparition of Mary, the mother of Jesus, on a hillside as they were gathering their sheep to bring them home. From that day to this, Mary is said to have appeared to some of these young people every day. They spend from one to six hours a day in prayer, along with the millions of pilgrims who have come to Medjugorje since. Few of those who have made the pilgrimage doubt that the prayers of millions of people for peace—for both spiritual and political freedom—have helped "to make ready for the Lord a people prepared" for peace and freedom, such as has come to Europe since the opening of the Berlin Wall.[1]

Peacemaking in East Germany.—The second happening that stands behind the democracy revolution in Eastern Europe also began in the early 1980s. Karl Friedrich Von Weizsacker, a noted physicist and leading Christian layman, called for a conciliar process leading to a call for peace by all the churches of East Germany.[2] The World Council of Churches picked up the call. Some denominations not a part of the World Council joined in, notably Baptists and Roman Catholics. The process and prayer for peace was nowhere more intense than in the churches of East Germany.

In East Germany, a consensus began to emerge as to specific

changes needed in the government. A twelve-part document, focused on justice demands, was circulated among the churches of all denominations for study and response. The suggestions in thousands of letters of response were then boiled down into a one-hundred-page document that was circulated to the churches. It received close attention in thousands of study groups for two years prior to the opening of the Berlin Wall. It was this process that enabled the leaders of the democracy revolution to move into the leadership vacuum with specific plans that represented a consensus among a large segment of the people.

Parallel to the conciliar process was the peacemaker movement in East Germany. These groups were active during the 1980s in linking worship and prayer with organization for peace and justice and training in nonviolent methods of social change. They developed a pattern of meeting in the churches for worship and prayer, then leaving the church where the worship was begun and walking silently to a church of a different denomination, carrying lighted candles. Usually, they would be intentional about walking across one or more bridges, symbolizing the bridging of differences between the churches. In the church to which they walked, the group would finish their worship experience.

The political context in which this happened was dictatorial and oppressive. Marches and protest were against the law. The peacemakers were allowed to conduct their walks only because they were defined as an integral part of ecumenical worship services. In the process, they developed patterns of organization and disciplined respect for their leaders that made it possible for them to conduct the nonviolent protest marches against the Communist Party's tyranny that brought down the government and opened the Berlin Wall in the closing months of 1989.

Conclusion

In the Jesus story, God breaks into the experience of a people who are politically oppressed by a superpower (Rome), but who are serious about their relationship to God. They have a mistaken idea about what God will do for them, as we see most clearly in the character called Lizzie. Most of Jesus' hearers and some of His followers were convinced to the end of His life that Jesus was going to bring in political freedom, economic prosperity, cultural glory, and make Israel number one among all the nations of the world. God's problem, therefore, was how to awaken the desire for a universal kingdom, a kingdom of justice and love, a realm in which the desire for God would be one with the desire to include all people—all races, cultures, and nations—in a spirit of hospitality and unbreakable good will.

God's strategy, as I see it in the opening move of the Jesus story, is to waken a desire for God that is also a desire for the kingdom of God "on earth as it is in heaven." To this end, it was necessary to make ready "a people prepared." Zechariah and Elizabeth, Mary and Joseph are prepared first with desire to be instruments of God. Their roles on the stage of history are not heroic by world standards. At one level they simply live life in an ordinary way. At an inner, spiritual level, they are "people prepared." They are prepared for their vision of the purposes of God to expand, their compassion to grow, until in Mary and the disciples of Jesus they embrace the whole human race.

What we see in the modern-day stories of Medjugorje and the conciliar process and peacemaker groups in East Germany suggests that the Jesus story continues in similar terms. When God breaks through into people's lives, individuals are made whole, at peace with themselves, one another, and with God; both they and those whom they influence become "a people prepared"—prepared for the public mission of setting free those who are oppressed, healing those who are broken, and with compassion, rather than with the methods of control, becoming instruments of peace.

In personal terms, these stories carry a caution. A strictly private experience of God is dangerous. It may become an escape from God or at best a strong temptation to resist the purposes of God in God's appearing to you. No experience is potentially more transforming than the unitive experience of a person with God. Let that experience isolate you from God's people, and you exchange God's gift for self-deception and illusion.

As you reflect on the stories in this chapter, you may wish to pray that familiar prayer of Saint Francis of Assisi, and to do so two times. First, pray it with the personal pronoun *me,* and second, with the inclusive pronoun *us.* As you learn to live with the collision of *me* and *us,* know that in doing so you are in company with Zechariah, Elizabeth, Mary, and Joseph, along with a countless host of characters in the Jesus story ever since.

> Lord, make me/us an instrument of Thy peace; where there is hatred, let me/us sow love; where there is injury, pardon; where there is doubt, faith; where there is despair, hope; where there is darkness, light; and where there is sadness, joy.

Notes

1. This information and much more is available from Weible Columns, Inc., P. O. Box 264, Myrtle Beach, S.C. 29578.

Because the happening at Medjugorje has become worldwide in scope, with pilgrims from all five continents, a formal report by the Croatian-speaking section of the Yugoslav Bishop's Conference has been released affirming the necessity of providing priests to assist the piigrims spiritually, to support the work of various domestic and foreign experts doing scientific investigations, and instructing priests not to speak about the messages of Medjugorje from the altar; neither are they to attack those events in the name of God and of the church as mendacious and diabolical. Priests and people are allowed to make pilgrimages individually or in privately organized groups. Finally, the report reminds the faithful that private revelations must be in accordance with public revelation, and that this judgment is the task of an official investigation by the Holy See which is underway. Until the results are known, the bishops counsel patience as well as the privilege of making pilgrimages. (Frane Franie, Archbishop of Split, *The Tablet*, 24 October 1987, 1167).

2. Such a call was first issued by the Baptist World Alliance, meeting in Berlin in 1934. Later the same year, Dietrich Bonhoeffer issued the same call to the German churches in an effort to contain or block Hitler's rearmament program. In neither case was the call taken seriously in the 1930s.

2

Awake to Adventure

"Awake to Adventure" carries a double meaning. It is both a call and a promise. Hear the word *awake* as the sound of a bugle blowing reveille! Hear the word *awake* as the call from Scripture, "It is now the moment for you to wake from sleep. For salvation is nearer to us now than when we became believers; the night is far gone, the day is near" (Rom. 13:11-12).

Remember the day you first publicly claimed the Jesus story as your story. Were you focused then on "adventure"? Or were you, like many others, more concerned to feel safe and secure, to belong to people who mattered, to get relief from a bad conscience by claiming God's forgiveness? After awhile, sometimes a long while, you heard the bugle calling you to a*wake to* a*dventure*! Then you understood Paul's word that "salvation is nearer to us now than when we first believed." Awakening to the Christian adventure is discovering that there is much beyond the rewards of your first believing.

The title, "Awake to Adventure," is also a promise. It describes a possible way of being in life, that is, being constantly aware (awake) of your life as an adventure. The Christian adventure is not just another journey to new places or meeting new people. It is not like being a tourist. Rather, it is a pilgrimage.

Adventure as Pilgrimage

A pilgrimage is not the same as a journey. A journey goes some place, from here to there. Your external world changes

while your internal world may remain the same. A pilgrimage
changes your internal world. You may well form new relationships with others who like yourself have found the door that
opens from the see-touch world into the unseen world of the
Holy Spirit. Together you waken to delights never experienced
before. Being awake to the Spirit of God is what matters most
on a pilgrimage.

As a pilgrim, you can never go back the way you came. The
world never looks the same again, because you are not the same.
You are traveling with a constant Companion. The inner Companion is called in Scripture "the *Paraclete*," which means one
who is called to one's side, who walks along with you. The *Paraclete* or Spirit of God speaks to you, entreats, consoles, encour-
ages, comforts, and instructs you. So a pilgrimage cannot be
done as a sleepwalk. Pilgrims are awake to the unseen world as
well as to the seen. Herein is life's greatest adventure.

In older times, people made pilgrimages to holy places. The
holy place might be a temple or a grove of trees, a river or a
mountain, a childhood home or a healing shrine. Pilgrims usually traveled together in companies. Often the pilgrimage was a
once-in-a-lifetime event. Pilgrims hoped to be met by the Holy
One in the holy place.

Today we might say that they hoped to become more centered, more at peace within, and more wholehearted. They
hoped to become more connected with the core of their inmost
selves. They believed that in leaving home for the holy place
they would find their true home. Going away was, then, the
way back.

While pilgrims often had grand ideas about the changes they
would experience once they reached the holy place, the pilgrimage itself was a mundane matter. It was a matter of finding
lodging, preparing food, avoiding robbers and tricksters along
the way, coping with storms, making decisions to throw away
excess baggage, and keeping their spirits up for the next rigorous day on the road.

You may want to make a pilgrimage today like those of long

ago. At best, you will plan ahead with ample time for soul-searching, both during the journey and at the holy place to which you travel. You will travel in the company of others who also understand the journey to be a pilgrimage and not just a vacation for tourists. You will go with the expectation and with planned opportunities for sharing your lives with one another, becoming vulnerable in sharing your fears and failures, your longings and hopes. You will sustain one another with the hope that in finding the Holy, you never again will be lost, adrift, confused about the meaning of life, or discouraged by the pain and losses that life inflicts. Being found by God, you will find your spiritual home, be connected with a loving company of fellow pilgrims, and together become a vital part of the Jesus story in your day.

Since the inner reality of pilgrimage is welcoming God into your inmost self, you do not need to leave your hometown ever. The journey is an interior one. Although it is best taken in the company of others who are also on pilgrimage, you need take only one small step from being asleep to the presence of God within to being awake to His presence. You continue to live in the ordinary world of the everyday. You suffer the hurts and disappointments of living with the same family members, neighbors, and working associates. You continue also to live with the same tensions, anxieties, contradictions, and craziness in yourself. So everything is the same, while everything is also different. What is different is that you are not alone. Emmanuel has come: "God with us." If you are on pilgrimage with a small group of companions, so much the better. What reassures you is that your desire is becoming centered now not on the lesser gods who demand addictive service, but on the God above gods whose perfect love gives you freedom to serve.

The Story of Jesus

Pilgrimage, as an interior journey, is lifelong. The Christian adventure, as pilgrimage, is a lifelong adventure. This is what we see in the story of Jesus. In this chapter we shall focus on the move from the manger to the temple. Jesus' birth is celebrated by an angelic choir appearing to nearby shepherds and by an astronomical wonder that caught the attention of astrologers from the East. The bugle sounded reveille to both the rural poor and the sophisticated rich. Some among both groups awoke! Then, like every other pious, Torah-obeying couple, Mary and Joseph brought the child to the temple for the rites of presentation (for circumcision) and purification forty days after the birth (for the mother).[1] In the events surrounding Jesus' birth and Mary's purification, we experience the tension between the personal and often private experience of awaking to the presence of God within and making public commitment to the story of God's people in history. The accent in the previous chapter was on the story, God's initiative in making "ready for the Lord a people prepared." The accent in this chapter is on awakening to the Spirit within. But the two cannot be separated in the Christian adventure. They are united like the center and the circumference of a circle.

The interconnections between personal awakening and public commitment to the Jesus story is the theme linking manger and temple. Next comes the story, as we await with Simeon and Anna the arrival of Jesus in the temple where the adventure begins.

Story: The Surprise

"Simeon, have your heard?" Anna called. Her voice was strong and clear for an old woman. You would never have guessed that she was in her eighties the way she rotated her canes to climb the temple stairs. Simeon waited for her on the landing as if he were standing at attention on the parade ground.

"What is it, Anna?"

"The shepherds," she panted. "Over a month ago now. They told our community that an angel of the Lord appeared to them in the fields. They said, 'In Bethlehem, a Savior was born.'

Called Him Messiah. Even told them where to find Him. The
night sky was full of angels singing,

> Glory to God in the highest heaven,
> and on earth peace among those
> whom he favors!"

"Now, Anna, are you sure this is not another one of your
visions?" Simeon's voice was always condescending.

"They went into Bethlehem that very night and found them.
She delivered in the manger behind the inn. They talked to
Joseph. Found out Joseph is Davidic. A carpenter up in Galilee
somewhere. Mother's name is Mary; just a girl. Her firstborn."

"Anna, you know I don't buy the Davidic line. At Qumran
we hold to the fundamentals—all the fundamentals, including
the Zadokite priesthood. The Messiah will come from the line
of Aaron!"

"Simeon, how long have you been an officer in the Wilderness Community at Qumran?"

"Twenty of my sixty-four years," he snapped.

"And Simeon, how many would-be messiahs have you cross-
examined for your community in those twenty years?"

"Why, maybe three or four hundred. Why does the prophetess ask? Surely you can see such things in your visions?" Simeon
struggled to get on the offensive with this tiny, old woman, but
her eyes had impaled him.

"Not one was authentic, right?" Anna's voice softened. "We
in the Jerusalem community have checked this one out thoroughly. They are a God-fearing, Torah-honoring couple,
Simeon. This child is nephew to Zechariah and Elizabeth. And
you, Simeon, are the officer that did the report for Qumran on
the boy John. That case is still under your investigation I suspect, or you would have gone back to the wilderness before
now."

"The report is finished. I take it back today, after morning
prayers." Anna waited in silence. "I give him a clean bill,
Anna."

"Simeon, Simeon! Delay your return just one day." Anna was excited now. "Wait with me in the temple this morning. We have determined that this is Mary's fortieth day. They are sure to bring the Child to the temple today for the rite of purification. You can meet them. You could even give them the priestly blessing, Simeon. The Baby is John's cousin. Your superiors will be pleased to have such a firsthand report from you. Surely word of the shepherds' claims has reached them already."

"All right, Anna. You win (as always)!" Simeon shifted his stance, as if his superior had said, "At ease." "Here, Anna, give me your arm, and I'll help you up the stairs.

The two of them lingered in the court of the Gentiles, waiting for Anna to spot the parents bringing the Child, Jesus. Anna enjoyed a reputation as a prophetess, which means that she had the gift of Sight. Mystic experience was not unknown in the wilderness community either, but Simeon as a man of action was afraid of it.

Simeon paced the temple court, checking the sundial, rubbing his arms and hands, and stopping occasionally to exchange a few words with Anna.

"I am uncommonly agitated, Anna. Your prediction about this Child must have gotten under my skin."

"Not my words, Simeon. The Spirit of God agitates a man."

Simeon stood still. He remembered something. Behind glazed eyes, he saw something out of his past. He grabbed at the pillar against which he and Anna stood. "Oh, my God! Could it be?" Simeon's eyes begged for help now. "I've never told a soul, Anna." The silence deepened. "Twenty-five years ago, while I was being initiated into the wilderness community, I had a vision. The Spirit revealed that I should not see death before I had seen the Messiah. In the vision, what I saw was . . . It . . . It was a baby! Do you suppose? Anna, could it be?"

"We shall soon see, Simeon. The family is entering the courtyard now." She nudged him toward his meeting with them.

Anna hung back, just in earshot, as Simeon introduced himself and offered to give the child the priestly blessing. As the blessing flowed out, Anna recognized the poetry of the Suffering Servant poems of Isaiah—passages central to the claims of the Jerusalem Poor Ones, anticipating a spiritual messianic kingdom. Anna grasped her throat, struggling for air. Simeon was inspired! His words were coming from beyond himself. The Spirit was in full charge!

> Master, now you are dismissing your servant in peace,
> according to your word;
> for my eyes have seen your salvation
> which you have prepared in the presence of all peoples,
> a light for revelation to the Gentiles
> and for glory to your people Israel (Luke 2:29-32).

Simeon blessed the parents. Then taking Mary aside he whispered something that Anna was unable to hear. Mary blanched, and Anna was certain that Simeon was still speaking in a trance.

Anna hobbled into the group, embraced Mary and the Baby, and gave thanks to God. Then taking Simeon by the hand, she led him out of the temple traffic where they could be alone.

"Anna," Simeon stammered, "Anna, He is the Lord, the Christ! He has come! He is here! I can die in peace."

"Can you, Simeon?" Anna held him in her eyes. "Are you at peace now, Simeon?"

"What do you mean? At peace? Yes . . . I mean, No . . . I mean, I don't know, Anna. I don't know."

"What did you say, Simeon, in the blessing: 'a light for revelation to the Gentiles' (Luke 2:32)? I was listening. You were in a trance, Simeon. Yes, that was your blessing. The Spirit spoke through you, beyond your knowing, against your believing. The Messiah comes for the Gentiles too.

"And then you pulled Mary aside and whispered to her. What did you see, Simeon? You had the Sight. What did the Spirit reveal to you then?"

"I saw . . . it . . . It rose out of the ground casting its shadow over the baby as I gave the blessing. It was a Roman cross! And then I saw the mother, Mary, crumpled on the ground at the foot of the cross."

"The mystery of suffering . . . " Anna echoed.

"Then *blackness* covered everything. An earthquake shook Jerusalem. The temple . . . the veils were torn in two, from top to bottom, exposing the holy of holies to public view!

Anna's litany continued: "The mystery of judgment . . ."

"I was compelled to tell her," Simeon cried, "This child is destined for the falling and the rising of many in Israel, and to be a sign that will be opposed so that the inner thoughts of many will be revealed—and a sword will pierce your own soul too" (Luke 2:34-35).

"The mystery of judgment in the gift of salvation . . ." Anna chanted her own responses in the liturgy of debriefing.

Placing her hand on Simeon's shoulder, Anna looked straight into his eyes and said: "And the 'sword' has pierced your own soul, Simeon! Now you must struggle with two mysteries: the mystery that God's Messiah is 'a light for revelation to the Gentiles' and the mystery of a messianic kingdom that is not about the politics of power but about a cross, the kingdom of a Suffering Servant. No, Simeon, you are not ready to die in peace. Not yet."

Comments on Story: The Surprise

The Action

The action of the story, "The Surprise," moves like traffic on a two-way street: Simeon is in one lane, Anna in the other, traveling in opposite directions. Simeon first discounts the news about the birth of Jesus but in the end accepts it, as he holds the child in his arms and pronounces the temple blessing. In the other lane, Anna moves steadily from excitement about the promise of Messiah's birth to the challenge of trying to open Simeon's closed mind. Simeon enters the story in control of his life. He leaves out of control. His world has been turned upside down. He is torn with inner conflict about the meaning of his sixty-four years, the cause he has served, and the vision that has drawn and driven him forward.

Simeon and Anna embodied generations of Israelites known as The Poor Ones. Simeon was a ranking officer of the community at Qumran, in the wilderness near the Dead Sea. Anna was a widow who for sixty-four years had given herself to the mystic disciplines of fasting and prayer night and day. She belonged to the Jerusalem community of The Poor Ones whose life centered in the temple.[2]

What these communities had in common was their conviction that they were the true remnant of Israel, keeping the faith in a coming Messiah. Where they differed was in the profile of the Messiah they awaited. The wilderness group looked for a Messiah who would take control of the centers of power and create a theocracy in strict fulfillment of the ancient laws of Moses. Readiness for military action was essential for the Poor Ones of the wilderness. Anna, and her community, stood in the prophetic tradition of Israel. The Poor Ones of Jerusalem looked for a spiritual transformation that might even penetrate the Gentile world. The temple was their center, providing a liturgy of prayers night and day.

The Characters

The characters of the story are many layered as well. At first look, this is a story about a man named Simeon. Anna is a supporting character, necessary only to draw out the story about the man. On reflection, we see that Anna becomes the heart and soul of the story. The current that carries both Simeon and Anna to their fateful meeting with Jesus comes from beyond them. Anna is aware. She cooperates with the cosmic tide. Simeon is threatened, trying with stubborn pride to hold back an ocean.

Simeon is an officer in a quasi-military religious sect based in the remote and rugged region around the Dead Sea. In his early forties he abandoned the world of ordinary occupations and family ties and received initiation into a sect known as The Poor

Ones of the wilderness. In contemporary experience, Simeon's move would be like entering a monastic order that is also active in an underground resistance movement against an empire ruling one's native land.

We see at once that Simeon is stoic, rigid in body, proud of his rational mind, and passionately loyal to his community's vision of the inherent superiority of Israel over all other peoples on earth. For the wilderness sect, Israel was God's chosen race, destined to rule the world at the coming of a militant messiah.

Simeon is disciplined not only as a soldier but also as a religious fanatic. The key to the hopes of The Poor Ones of the wilderness was their zeal in keeping the Mosaic law, the Torah. Their reward for strict obedience would be the gift of power— power to rule over "all the kingdoms of the world" (Matt. 4:8). It is not surprising that Jesus, who knew the religious culture of The Poor Ones of the wilderness, should have faced the ultimate temptation (in "the wilderness") to rule "all the kingdoms of the world" and to enjoy "the glory of them." What Jesus saw as a temptation from Satan, Simeon and the entire wilderness community served with dogmatic passion as the will of God.[3]

The story began with a minor complication in Simeon's life: Anna's excitement about the birth of a Baby. It moved to a major complication, namely, Simeon's surrender of himself to that same Baby as the promised Messiah. He gave up his obsession with power to embrace a future that was stamped already with the omen of a Roman cross, humiliation, and defeat. How could this be? What forces were at work? From a literary point of view, we cannot help but wonder if the transformation of Simeon is believable.

To answer this question, we must pay attention to the woman in the story: Anna. Notice that Anna appears to be important only in trying to understand Simeon. The story takes place in a man's world, so, of course, the woman is subordinate.

Yet Anna has the first word and the last in the story. She enters as a woman in her eighties, energetically climbing the temple stairs with the help of her canes. We sense at once that

Anna is no ordinary mortal. We feel her excitement about the shepherd's story, but hers is not the intensity of hysteria. She has done her homework. The facts about this birth have been dug out. Anna knows that she has a viable messianic candidate in her sights. They fit the profile of The Poor Ones of Jerusalem, the monastic community to which she belongs.

Like an experienced trial lawyer, Anna takes on the rigid, proud, and condescending officer of their rival community, The Poor Ones of the wilderness. With two razor-sharp questions, she opened up Simeon to his own disillusionment about the wilderness community's messianic vision. For over twenty years, Simeon has written up official reports on nearly four hundred would-be messiahs in Israel, yet not one was found to be authentic. Anna, in contrast, ticks off the criteria for genuineness. The baby Jesus passes the test according to the criteria in use by the Jerusalem Poor Ones. She waits silently while Simeon confesses that he carries at that moment a final report on "baby John" (John the Baptist), a report that will lend credence to Jesus even in the wilderness community.

Immediately Anna swings into action again, but without the trial lawyer approach. Her voice is alive with desire and hospitality for Simeon. She is not above manipulation, appealing to Simeon's self-interest as a career officer; but her achievement is not in "winning," as Simeon says, but in relaxing the warrior. As they move on up the temple stairs to the court of the Gentiles, the way has been prepared for Simeon's transformation. Anna knows it is so.

From here on, the central character of the story is the Spirit of God. Anna understands this. The Spirit wakens Simeon to remember the one and only vision experience he may have had: a peak experience during his initiation into The Poor Ones of the wilderness. The promise that he would not die until he had seen the long-awaited Messiah came in a vision of a baby boy.

Then the baby Jesus arrived with Mary and Joseph. The possibilities of this moment overwhelm Simeon. He functions from this point on in a state of high inspiration, seeing and saying

48   THE CHRISTIAN ADVENTURE

things beyond his conscious knowing. What he says and what
he sees shatter all of his preconceived ideas of what God is
about in the world. Anna knows. She knows that Simeon will
never be at peace until he surrenders fully to the vision he has
received. She knows that his racial and religious superiority
feelings have splintered under the impact. She knows that his
grandiose fantasy of Israel ruling the world is crumbling. She
knows, as she said, " 'the sword' has pierced your own soul,
Simeon."

We sense that Anna knows even more, more than she can tell
within the scope of the story. She knows that crucifixion is both
history and metaphor about the meaning of life. In the end we
know that although Simeon is the dominant character of the
story, Anna is more potent. Anna, the shriveled up old woman,
stands taller than Simeon: wiser by far, more powerful with her
eyes than Simeon with his muscles, and truly godlike in her
heart.

The Themes

Moving from reflection on the plot and characters to theme,
the story is a parable for all times. The theme has to do with the
Divine breaking into human history and into personal experience. In history, the vision of God most to be trusted is nourished by the group most in touch with "the poor ones" of the
earth. The personal religious experience closest to the mark is
that which arises from the feminine dimensions of the soul.
Across both the corporate and personal realms of life lies the
shadow of a Roman cross. In "The Surprise," all of these
themes burst open, yet remain veiled in mystery. Simeon is not
ready to die in peace. Says Anna, "Not yet."

Desire for God

The God-image Factor

Simeon's desire is for a warrior God. Anna sees God in a
newborn Baby. Then Simeon remembers that the high point of

his spiritual life came in a vision of a baby—born to be Messiah. And Simeon begins to wonder. He must work through many questions, such as why he assumed that Messiah meant "power" rather than love; why a warrior rather than a "Suffering Servant"? Why he built his beliefs on the prophecies of militant might rather than those of humiliation and service? Why he ignored the central symbol of the vision: a newborn baby?

What is it about Anna that enabled her to find fulfillment of her desire for God in a Baby? Is it because she is woman and not man? Or is it that as a woman she has lived among the oppressed of her culture? She has known what it is to be passed from her father to a husband in her twelfth year, without voice; to be married without legal rights, subject to divorce without appeal, defense, or property; to be widowed without name or place in the society; even to be excluded from the holy place in the temple, relegated to the court for women and foreigners. As woman, Anna was valued mainly for her biological functions. As widow, she lost even that reason for being. As woman, she was victim of the rule makers, the God explainers, and the warriors of her race.

Is it any wonder that Anna found her hope wakened in Isaiah's vision of a Messiah who "was despised and rejected by others; / a man of suffering and acquainted with infirmity"; a Messiah who "was oppressed, and . . . afflicted, / yet he did not open his mouth; / like a lamb that is led to the slaughter (Isa. 53:3,7)?

Yet Simeon and Anna are both identified with monastic communities dedicated to The Poor Ones. Why did desire for God take root in the primary desires for safety and security and grow into the worship of power for one, while the other's desire for God was grounded in the primary desires for belonging and esteem and flowered in unconditional love? Why were spiritual disciplines devoted to conquest for the one and to sacrificial service in the other? Why did the radical obedience of one create a rigid, dogmatic, harsh, and bitter person, while for the other, the same measure of obedience fashioned a gentle, patient, open-minded, wise, and nourishing person?

These questions force a closer look at desire for God. Desire for God takes many forms. It enslaves, and it frees. From infancy, desire for safety and desire for survival emerge alongside desire for attachment and for belonging. One feeds the other, and God is in them all. Almost at once, desire for adventure, for exploration, and desire for the familiar—for returning home— appear. Then desire to stretch, grow, and change begins to wrestle with desire to shrink back and be content with old habits. As we grow, conflict among desires sharpens. With desire we destroy, and with desire we create. With desire we bond to others, and with desire we break promises and betray commitments; with desire we love, and with desire we hate. With desire we try to capture God in the service of all of our desires.

Like Simeon, then, our desire for God may serve mainly our needs for safety and security without being balanced by our needs for belonging, esteem, and love. Combined with the fear that we are alone in the universe, that it is up to us to control our own destiny, our desires feed a lust for power.

Like Anna, our desire for God may serve our needs for belonging, for esteem, and more. The *more* is our need to welcome God within the core of our being, to allow awareness of God to be born in us—small and weak like a baby—but very much alive. Then our own Anna-like self wakes and begins to grow within us. We can relax our need to be in absolute control. We can give ourselves to love with generosity and abandon. We discover the capacity to create community built on justice and love. Best of all, we discover that our wills and our desires are becoming one. Our desire for God shapes our wills for ourselves until the desire for God is at one with God's desire for us.

Seeing the Sacred in the Everyday

Another contrast between Simeon and Anna has to do with seeing the sacred in the ordinary events of every day. Simeon was focused on the future; Anna, on the present. Simeon expected something dramatic, a superman performance that would compel the masses to follow. Anna expected God to appear in the unlikely places (such as a manger in Bethlehem), to slip quietly and humbly into the world, and to be inclusive of women as well as men, slaves as well as masters, sinners as well as the self-righteous, and Gentiles as well as the "chosen" people. She wanted a Messiah who could see and care about people like herself, all the little people on the fringe of the earth. Simeon was looking for power; Anna, for love.

The apostle Paul struggled against the wish to make a big deal out of spirituality in the church at Corinth. In the famous "love chapter" (1 Cor. 13), Paul challenged the spirituality of grand words: "If I speak in the tongues of mortals and of angels, but do not have love, I am a noisy gong or a clanging cymbal."

Next, Paul took on clairvoyance, mystic wisdom, and specialized graduate education: "And if I have prophetic powers, and understand all mysteries and all knowledge."

"Psychic powers" and prayer healing were next to collapse under Paul's assault on "big deal" spiritual gifts: "and if I have all faith, so as to remove mountains, but do not have love, I am nothing."

Asceticism, such as vows of poverty, and even martyrdom come under Paul's pruning knife: "If I give away all my possessions, and if I hand over my body so that I may boast, but do not have love, I gain nothing."

Not even the "big deal" goals of contemporary spirituality—namely, wellness, wholeness, and integration—survive, unless they are based on the primacy of "faith, hope, [and] love," recognizing that "the greatest of these is love."

In context, Paul's agenda for the "on fire" members of the church at Corinth was to help them see that all the "big deal" forms of spirituality were "childish ways." So, he said, "I will show you a still more excellent way" (1 Cor. 12:31).

Relaxation, Not Argument

Anna provides another clue to seeing the sacred in the every-day. She helps Simeon to be "at ease" rather than to get into an argument with him about their different theories concerning the Messiah. Nothing is more basic to nurturing your desire for God than good habits of relaxation. Body tension restricts your vision to the see-touch world, limits your awareness to a narrow range, and reinforces old habits of holding yourself under tight mental and emotional control.

Anna models a level of relaxation beyond the physical, how-ever. After morning prayers, as Simeon is pacing the temple courtyard, he complains, "I am uncommonly agitated, Anna. Your prediction about this Child has gotten under my skin." Anna responds, "Not my words, Simeon. The Spirit of God agi-tates a man." Then it happened. Simeon became open to an in-ternal dialogue with God.

Anna relaxed her need to be the one who would open Si-meon's eyes to the mysteries they were about to face in the birth of Jesus. She relaxed her need to play god. She could do this because she was convinced in her heart that the Spirit of God was at work; He is always at work, pursuing people, bringing them to the point of seeing the sacred in the common events before their eyes.

A Sword Piercing the Soul

Finally, we may learn from Anna to pay attention to those moments when "a sword" pierces the soul—whether the soul of another with whom we are engaged or our own souls. Simeon's vision, as he held the baby Jesus, was a vision of Jesus' death on a Roman cross. The sword of truth about this Jesus and His messiahship pierced Simeon's soul first. Then he could not but prophesy that it would pierce the soul of Mary as well.

The ultimate mystery about God entering the world in the person of Jesus is not that God became a man. Mythical stories of nearly every culture on earth tell of gods becoming human.

The mystery is not that the God above gods became a man. This claim tends to conceal the mystery by stimulating arguments that can never be won by any religion. The darkest mystery of all about the Jesus story is that the one and only God, the Creator of all things, not only became a man, but died as a common criminal in the most humiliating way ever devised by the evil imagination of the race. Nothing could have been more shocking, less believable, or more abhorrent to the people of Jesus' day in Israel than to entertain the thought that God might be executed on a Roman cross.[4]

The desire for God is a dangerous desire. Simeon discovered it in a revelation direct from God. Mary's soul was pierced with the truth of it by Simeon's word. Only Anna was prepared for it. You and I now have a sober reminder that the awakening of desire for God is like "a sword" piercing the "soul." This is the drumbeat that sets the rhythm for the Jesus story from beginning to end. No sooner is the Child born than the shadow of the cross falls across His crib. No sooner does a person waken to the desire for God than that person's ego is put on the defensive. To have the "mind" of Christ, as Paul put it in Philippians 2:5-8, is to become "obedient to the point of death— / even death on a cross." Could it be that this is what God is about in the world and what the Jesus story is about for each one of us who voluntarily enters that story and plays out our part in the ordinariness of our everyday lives?

The story of Simeon and Anna is, indeed, "*The* Surprise." It uncovers a surprise that will keep on startling us as we move on in succeeding chapters to the marker events in the life of the Baby who, like a sword, will pierce the soul of all who believe His incredible claims: the claim that He and God are one, and the even more preposterous claim, that in Him, God is nailed to a Roman cross to die.

Notes

1. Raymond E. Brown, *The Birth of the Messiah: A Commentary on the Infancy Narratives in Matthew and Luke* (Garden City, N.Y.: Doubleday & Company, Inc., 1977).

2. For an early analysis of the wilderness community of The Poor Ones see, Albert Gelin, *The Poor of Yahweh*, trans. K. Sullivan (Collegeville, Minn.: Liturgical Press, 1964).

3. Data supporting this interpretation is thoroughly documented in the following: Ethelbert Stauffer, *Jesus and the Wilderness Community at Qumran*, Biblical Series, no. 10, trans. Hans Spaltehaly (Philadelphia: Fortress Press, Facet Books, 1964).

4. The theme is documented in the following: Martin Hengel, *Crucifixion in the Ancient World and the Folly of the Message of the Cross* (Philadelphia: Fortress Press, 1977).

3

Beyond the Point of No Return

Jesus was a true son of Israel when He came to the time for His bar mitzvah. The story of His encounter with His parents in the temple is a marker event, a point of no return. Similarly, His baptism marks a point of no return. In both of these events, Jesus declared Himself to be committed to the Torah and the temple as the foundation and center of the faith into which He was born and reared.

As Jesus launched His own ministry apart from John the Baptist, He moved beyond the point of no return. He set out to violate the Jewish religious leaders' interpretation of the Torah and to reject the temple as the only place to worship. With clear vision and determination He went beyond the pale—breaking through the fences, crossing the boundary of conventional religion, violating the tradition, and moving against the stream.

Why, we must ask, did Jesus break away from John the Baptist? Why did He intentionally violate the prevailing understandings of the Hebrew Scriptures in which He was reared? Why did He separate Himself from the reform movement into which He was baptized? What was it that led Him beyond the tradition He had received, even beyond the rigorous effort of John the Baptist to purify that tradition? Why did Jesus sacrifice His reputation as a true son of Israel, a young man of wisdom, "in divine and human favor" (Luke 2:52), and become a radical, an agent of change—stirring "up the people," inviting the charge of "perverting our nation" (Luke 23:2-5)? Why did

He provoke the doctors of the law to conclude that He was possessed of Satan and His own mother and brothers to try to seize
Him, saying, "He has gone out of his mind" (Mark 3:21)?

What does it say to us today—those of us who are on the
Christian adventure, who make a commitment that takes us
across the point of no return religiously—then to be driven beyond that point of no return? These are the questions that shape
the discussion and the story that follow. Consider first the context of the story, then, the story, "A Night Visitor," and finally,
some concluding comments and applications.

The Context of Conflict

The years between Jesus' birth and infancy and the beginning
of His public ministry are called the hidden years. Scripture
provides only one glimpse of Jesus growing up. Luke reported
that Jesus' parents went to Jerusalem every year at the Feast of
the Passover. When Jesus was twelve years old, His parents discovered that He was not in the group of kinsfolk and acquaintances who were returning to Galilee. They returned to Jerusalem looking for Him and found Him in the temple, "sitting
among the teachers, listening to them and asking them questions." Luke also noted that the Jerusalem rabbis "were amazed
at his understanding and his answers."

Mary scolded Him, saying, "Son, why have you treated us
so?" Jesus answered: "Why were you searching for me? Did
you not know that I must be in my Father's house?" The scene
ends with Jesus returning to Nazareth with them, being "obedient to them" (Luke 2:41-52).

Luke wrote his Gospel for Gentile Christians at least fifty
years after Jesus' death and resurrection and a decade or more
after the destruction of Jerusalem by the Roman army. It was
important, therefore, to show the Gentile readers that the Jewish law (the Torah) and the temple were central in Jesus' development. He showed, also, that at the age of twelve, the traditional year for a Jewish boy to become a full adult member of
the nation Israel, Jesus declared His primary loyalty to His

Heavenly Father and His commitment to Judaism as represented in the temple.

The formal education of a Jewish boy at the time of Jesus began at age five. The father began then to train his son in the Torah. At age ten, if a synagogue school were available, instruction in the Torah was intensified along with the learning of the tradition. A boy was expected to know the whole law of Yahweh and to practice its requirements by age thirteen. He was then legally of age, entitled to enter the court of the Israelites (for Jewish men only). By age fifteen, a select few boys went to Jerusalem for a higher level of religious studies. Such a school was the *beth ha-midrash*, taught by famous doctors of the law, such as Gamaliel with whom the young Saul of Tarsus studied. It is doubtful that Jesus attended one of these schools, but likely that His brother, James, who will appear in the story that follows, was studying for the rabbinate in such a school during the time of Jesus' public ministry.

The Torah provided the foundation of religious education for Jewish piety, fidelity, and respect for tradition. In the scene before us, we see Jesus growing up in the tension between obedience to a tradition He knew well and the independence and inner freedom to question that tradition and to probe its deeper meanings in dialogue with rabbis and doctors of the law.

Eighteen years pass before we have another glimpse into the life of Jesus. At age thirty, a Jewish man was qualified to become a rabbi, a teacher. Before thirty, a person could not presume to possess wisdom. At thirty, therefore, Jesus entered the stage of history, seeking baptism at the hand of John "in the wilderness" (Luke 3:2).

Strong evidence suggests that John the Baptist may have been a member at one time of The Poor Ones of the wilderness, the community in which Simeon was a member (as I portrayed him in the previous chapter). Jesus, too, may have spent time in such a wilderness community prior to making the commitment to join the reform movement under John's leadership. Since Jesus was not married, it is unlikely that He could have received a hearing at all unless He had committed Himself to such a community. Jewish law required the eldest son to assume responsibility for the family in the event of the father's death. An exception could be made only if the firstborn son were "married to the Law" through becoming a rabbi or joining a prophetic community.[1]

In any event, Jesus' baptism was a refinement and focusing of His commitment as a son of Israel. Also, it was a symbolic event marking the crossing of a point of no return. In the temple at twelve and in the wilderness baptism at thirty, Jesus took His stand as an informed, serious, and reform-minded believer in the tradition of Moses and the Prophets.

John the Baptist differed from the wilderness community in several ways. Both sought to cleanse and purify the nation by demanding the strictest possible obedience to the Torah. For John, this also meant wholehearted integrity and devotion to both God and neighbor. John demanded a life-style of high ethical conduct as well as strict ritual purity according to the Torah. The driving power of his message was that strict obedience to the Law was necessary to prepare for the Messiah who was coming. Unlike the wilderness community, John had an inclusive vision. He announced the coming of a Messiah in whom "all flesh [would] see the salvation of God." He required "fruits worthy of repentance" and declared to those who felt secure in their Jewish heritage that "God is able from these stones to raise up children to Abraham." "Even now," he warned, "the ax is lying at the root of the trees; every tree therefore that does not bear good fruit is cut down and thrown into the fire" (Luke 3:3-9).

John not only differed with the wilderness community, he offended them. By going to the common people and calling them to repentance, he undercut the pretensions of those in the wilderness communities who claimed that only they were capable of keeping the law perfectly. By requiring baptism, he offended Jews of every class and party. Baptism was a ritual normally used only for Gentiles who were converting to Judaism.

John's baptism, therefore, required the Jews to confess that they were no better than the Gentiles before God, unless they came to repentance, kept the law, and offered genuine worship to God.

The Gospels reveal a close connection between John the Baptist and Jesus prior to Jesus' public ministry. The Fourth Gospel reports that some of the Galileans among John's disciples began to shift their allegiance to Jesus. John himself seems to have introduced his disciples to Jesus. He and His first disciples then left Judea where John was working, returned to Galilee, and called some other Galileans into His service.

Within a few weeks, Jesus and His group were on their way to Jerusalem for the Passover. At the celebration Jesus carried out a protest action against corruption in the temple, driving out the money changers (John 2:13-22). It must have been similar to a protest march today. It is not known why the temple police did not swing into action against Jesus. The Jewish law forbade any disturbance of temple activities.

Of special interest is the likelihood that Jesus became a public figure leading this protest action during a Passover feast. He would have received maximum publicity among the people and become marked as a dangerous radical to be watched by the temple hierarchy and their police forces as well as by the other major political parties in Jerusalem.

At the same time, tension was growing between the followers of John and Jesus. Two issues appear: the issue of ritual purity according to the Torah and rivalry over the number of people being baptized. Apparently, Jesus was not keeping the law as some felt He should, and His disciples were baptizing more people than John's (see John 3:25-30).

On the way home from the Passover, Jesus went through Samaria, talked with the Samaritan woman and stayed in her village for two days, teaching the people. Of special interest here is the dialogue that evoked Jesus' words:

> Woman, believe me, the hour is coming when you will worship
> the Father neither on this mountain nor in Jerusalem. . . . But
> the hour is coming, and is now here, when the true worshipers
> will worship the Father in spirit and truth, for the Father seeks
> such as these to worship him. God is spirit, and those who wor-
> ship him must worship in spirit and truth" (John 4:21-24).

Hints of big changes appear. Jesus violated tradition in speaking to a woman, any woman, but especially to a Samari-tan. He crossed the boundaries of male dominance and of racial superiority. Most important to this discussion, Jesus took a stand against the basic passion of His nation in saying that the worship of God transcends the temple and all that the temple represents.

His next stop was Cana in Galilee where He changed the wa-ter into wine at a wedding. This was the kind of activity that prompted Jesus' critics to call Him a "drunkard."

Jesus then concentrated His energies in Galilee for two or three months. Everything reported in the Gospels during these months could have taken place within a few days or two weeks at most. "After this," we read, "there was a festival of the Jews, and Jesus went up to Jerusalem" (John 5:1).

At this unnamed feast in Jerusalem, in the face of the most strict doctors of the law and rulers of the temple, Jesus began to violate the Torah on purpose. He healed the man at the pool of Beth-zatha who had been ill for thirty-eight years. Jesus com-manded the man, "Stand up, take your mat and walk." And the text reads: "Now that day was a sabbath" (John 5:8-9).

The man was chronically ill. He had been incapacitated for thirty-eight years. Jesus would be in Jerusalem for at least a week. He had no need to heal this person on the Sabbath, nor to require Him to carry His pallet and walk on the Sabbath. Both were direct and flagrant violations of Sabbath law. Clearly, Jesus intended to break the law and by doing so to get the atten-tion of the religious leaders as well as the people. Jesus' purpose was to engage them in learning about the kingdom of God, and to reveal His own authority as the Son of God, acting on the authority of the Father.

The man told the religious rulers who healed him, and the text reads: "Therefore the Jews started persecuting Jesus, because he was doing such things on the sabbath." As Jesus explained Himself to them, their opposition increased. And again the text reads: "For this reason the Jews were seeking all the more to kill him, because he was not only breaking the sabbath, but was also calling God his own Father, thereby making himself equal to God" (John 5:16,18).

In reviewing the sequence of events in Jesus' public ministry to this point, we have traced the widening gulf between Jesus and John the Baptist and concluded with the enraged religious leaders in Jerusalem plotting Jesus' death. Now we see Jesus going beyond the point of no return by standing against the very tradition in which He was clearly identified.

The question that begs to be addressed next is, Why? Why did Jesus go beyond His commitment to the Hebrew Scripture and religious tradition, to the Torah and the temple? Why did He part ways with John the Baptist, His cousin, friend, and companion in His own spiritual life? Why did He back away from the strict legalism of John and the fanatical messianic doctrine that was at the heart of the wilderness community?

To answer these questions we must turn to the marker event in Jesus' life that we have ignored to this point, that is, the temptations in the wilderness. The phrase "the wilderness" does not mean empty space. In the context of baptism at the hand of John the Baptist, the "wilderness" connotes a region that was the heart of the messianic movement in Israel. The temptations describe an inner struggle with the issues that were central to those wilderness communities. It was Jesus' victory over the devil in the temptation scene that set Him on a collision course with the religious leadership of His day.

The fundamentals of the faith of Israel were symbolized in the three temptations: the bread, the mountain, and the temple. The manna with which God fed the people in the desert, the

62   THE CHRISTIAN ADVENTURE

mountain on which Moses received the Commandments, and
the temple around which the entire society was to be organized—all had become literal, material, and political realities.

The Messiah, therefore, would usher in an age of material
prosperity, like turning the stones of the desert into bread. A
messianic empire would be established that would require strict
and literal obedience to the entire code of laws derived from the
Mosaic legacy. It would impose these laws—both of ritual purity and of ethical integrity—on all the nations of the world.
Worship in the messianic age would center in the Jerusalem
temple, believed to be the center of the earth, and the final arbi-
ter of all things. These were the enticements of the messianic
vision in the wilderness communities out of which John the
Baptist came. But these became the masks and garments worn
by the devil seeking to deceive Jesus as He shaped the unique
vision of His mission as the Messiah of Israel, the Son of God.

Jesus saw through the shallow, magical, and self-serving interpretations of Scripture that prevailed in the religious climate
of His time. He could not tolerate for long the grandiose messianic expectations of the wilderness communities. Even though
he respected John and shared John's witness to ethical courage
and integrity, Jesus also differed with John as to the kind of
Messiah He was. He totally rejected the literal interpretations
of Scripture that abounded. He saw the materialistic and
power-hungry fantasies that were built into the very fabric of
the law and of temple worship. These fantasies were garments
of the devil rather than the word and worship of God. "God is
spirit," He told the Samaritan woman, "and those who worship
him must worship in spirit and truth" (John 4:24).

It was "in the wilderness," in the midst of the most rigorous
and zealous religionists of the land, that Jesus set a course that
would take Him beyond the earlier point of no return, beyond
the Torah and the temple, beyond John the Baptist and popular
messianic expectations. His was the new wine of a new covenant. He was nurtured in the old and honored it. But as He
launched His public ministry apart from John the Baptist, Jesus

threw aside the old wineskins of legalism and nationalistic patriotism. He lived and taught the joyful, compassionate life of the Spirit—the Spirit of an inclusive, forgiving, truth-loving, and transforming God.

The story that follows takes place soon after Jesus returned to Galilee and just prior to His going back to Jerusalem for the Feast of Tabernacles. Except for occasional trips to Jerusalem for high holy days, He and His disciples remained in Galilee for about a year and a half prior to His final journey to Jerusalem. As the story opens, He is riding a crest of popular excitement in Capernaum where He and His disciples have established their headquarters.

Story: A Night Visitor

"But, Mother, I'm telling you, He's gone mad!" James, the brother of Jesus, was fighting to save his brother's life.

"Now, James, you're talking nonsense," Mary replied. "You of all people know how obedient Jesus was to the Torah when He was with you in Nazareth."

"I'm telling you God's truth, Mother. Since Jesus left John the Baptist and came back here to Galilee, He has intentionally and flagrantly violated the Torah at every turn."

"Jesus is a true son of Israel, James, and so are you. But you've got to remember, He is still a Galilean! Galileans are free spirits, James. You know that. It's you who have changed. Maybe you should not have stayed in Jerusalem after completing your studies with Rabbi Gamaliel."

"Mother!" James was struggling against his despair of overcoming his mother's favoritism for her firstborn. "Can't you see what is happening? Jesus is allowing those Galilean ruffians of His to pluck grain and eat it—on the Sabbath! That violates the Torah! It is punishable by death!

"They eat with hands defiled. That violates the Law! It is punishable by death.

"He recruited that Roman collaborator—Matthew. That

makes Him a disobedient son of Israel. It is punishable by death.

"On His way back from Passover, He traveled through Samaria. He talked with a Samaritan woman. And, as if that were not bad enough, He stayed in their village for two days, and, of course, He ate with them. You know yourself, He has been to Tyre and to Sidon lately. He was seen publicly talking with a Gentile woman. Jesus is now a disobedient son of Israel. It is punishable by death.

"Do you get the picture, Mother? Your son is beside Himself. He has lost His judgment. He is on a collision course with all that you and Father have taught us to respect as sacred. So is He a heretic, or is He mad? If He is a heretic, He will be stoned to death. If He is mad, we may be able to find a way to save His life!" The silence grew heavy.

Mary got up, rearranged the pottery on the counter, and said, "Why are you telling me these things, James?"

"Because you, Mother, are the only one He will listen to."

Mary fought back the hurt and anger she felt remembering the scene when Jesus announced that He was leaving Nazareth to check out the wilderness community and John the Baptist. She heard James' voice echoing in her ears: "Mother, you must not agree to Jesus' craziness. He should marry, bring His wife home, and take His place as head of the family, now that Father is gone. You, Mother, are the only one He will listen to." Instead, she had agreed that James would take his place. Since Jesus was officially "marrying the law," He was freed from His duties to marry a woman and assume responsibility for His mother and siblings. *But,* she wondered, *did I make a mistake? Would it have come to this if Jesus had married and stayed in Nazareth?*

Finally, Mary turned back to James and asked, "So what do you suggest?"

James then outlined his plan for saving Jesus from a heretic's death. Mary was to come to Capernaum with James, persuade Jesus to return with them to Nazareth for some much-needed rest and relaxation. Once back home, Mary would support James in negotiating a betrothal. James, then, would return to Jerusalem and negotiate with the Pharisees and scribes to drop their charges against Jesus on the grounds of temporary insanity.

"You see," James concluded, "before Jesus split with John the Baptist, He had a lot of friends among the Pharisees. We all thought He was true blue in defense of the Torah and for a purified temple. In fact, He led our protest action against the money changers in the temple just a few months ago during Passover. The prophet's movement is still strong enough in Judea that we can checkmate the Sadducees in the council. And I can convince the Pharisees that it will be to their advantage to have Jesus up here in Galilee supporting the reform movement.

"I'm sure they will go along once they see that Jesus is settling down. Marriage will convince them that He is a true son of Israel once again, who is honoring you by bringing a wife into your home to care for you."

But Mary turned away, saying, "I don't know, James, I just don't know."

The next morning, however, she told James, "I can't do it. I just cannot do it. When Jesus left home, we all agreed that He would not marry and that you, James, would assume your father's place in our family. There's no turning back." With outstretched arms that were both pleading for James to understand and yielding to the mystery she had always sensed surrounding Jesus, she concluded, "He has crossed a point of no return. It is in God's hands now."

"No," James said to himself, "Jesus has gone *beyond* the point of no return. And that's the problem!"

The next day James presented Mary with a second plan. "We will go to Capernaum together, talk with Jesus the way we did when He was considering joining John the Baptist, and urge Him to return to Judea and take the leadership of the movement, now that John is in prison."

James was persuasive. He assured Mary that as head of the

movement Jesus could take His healing power right to the heart of the nation and enjoy the protection of some prominent Pharisees who were strongly supportive of the Baptist's cause. So, on this basis, Mary agreed to go with James to talk the plan over with Jesus.

Preparations for the trip were quickly made, and they set out for Capernaum where Jesus and His disciples had their home base. It was a bright spring day, but the symphony of greens in the field and trees were a dirge of greys to James that day. His eyes saw only the specter of enraged rabbis stoning his brother to death. He saw them drawing their robes around themselves and pulling away from him as well. In his inner ear he could hear them saying, "James is the brother of that Galilean heretic, you know. You can't trust a Galilean to stand firm as a true son of Israel. No matter how hard they try to pass as one of us, they are all a bunch of rebels under the skin."

James had no problem finding the headquarters building. As they came in sight of Capernaum, the road became jammed with people on their way to the Healer. They could tell that some were handicapped, lame, or blind. Others, they were told, suffered from fevers, consumption, epilepsy, or dropsy. Some were deaf, and others, dumb. All were full of excitement and hope because of the stories they had heard of healings and even of exorcisms.

As they passed one cluster of folks, they heard someone say, "I'll tell you how He does those healings! He forgives sins, that's how. Once your sins are forgiven, the demons have no more power over you. And," someone added, "you don't even have to go down to Jerusalem to the temple and get robbed paying for a sacrificial lamb." James broke out in a cold sweat at the thought of how his Jerusalem colleagues would react to the news that Jesus was forgiving sins!

James got Mary settled at the inn and hurried back to the headquarters, hoping to arrange a leisurely afternoon with his boyhood friends, reliving the old days before trying to win them over to his plan. He found the Zebedee brothers at the edge of the crowd directing traffic. He realized at once that there would be no leisurely evening with any of the disciples. He and Mary would be lucky to get a few minutes with Jesus the next day. He would have to talk with the Zebedee boys on the move. He would have to hit them straight if he were to get their attention in this chaos. Fortunately, however, he had come upon two of the disciples whom he knew from his boyhood in Galilee. He was sure that they had Jesus' ear.

So James shuttled back and forth between the two of them as they directed the crowds. He told them what he had already said to Mary about the danger of an inquisition from Jerusalem and of a heretic's death for Jesus.

For James it was like blowing soap bubbles in the air. All he got in response were discounts, threats, and questions about his own integrity. As he left the crowds to return to his lodgings for the night, he replayed their words:

"Hey, man, we've got too much going here in Galilee."

"Can't you see the crest we're riding? Why should we hook up with the losers in Judea?"

"Your kind want to go backward toward the old covenant. We are going forward into a new covenant."

"Let the inquisitors come with their temple police. We've got protection from our friends in the hills—if you know what I mean!" The gestures of a slit throat removed all doubt about what they meant. Everyone was aware of the brigands in the caves of the Galilee hill country, especially their victims, who kowtowed to the temple hierarchy and collaborated with Rome.

And the cruelest cut of all: "So you came all the way up here to Galilee just to protect your own career in Jerusalem?"

"I guess it could be hard to get ahead in that Jerusalem crowd when you're the brother of the prophet Jesus."

When James reached the inn, he found it filled by a delegation of scribes and the temple police who came with them from Jerusalem. The leader of the delegation was a former teacher of James during his early years in *beth ha-midrash*. He was the strictest of the doctors of the law, short of stature, but intimidating in an argument, merciless with the student who had not memorized all of the fine points of a lesson.

Mary was content to spend the evening alone resting from their trip. It was important for James to reintroduce himself to the great doctor from Jerusalem. He needed help and guidance. Here in his former teacher he would find the answer he was hunting.

James quickly made it clear to the doctor that he was in Capernaum trying to dissuade Jesus from allowing His followers to violate the law. The doctor was delighted to have this young man in his clutches, all the more so because he was the brother of Jesus. Lubricated with wine and inflated with his own prominence among the peasants of Palestine, the doctor patronized James with his interpretations and advice about "this Jesus thing."

"Now this Jesus thing looks good on the surface," the doctor said as he began his monologue. "He teaches absolute love for everybody, including your enemies. But who are your enemies, young man? The Romans, of course. And why are they our enemies? Because they make Caesar a god. They do not merely make graven images as did the Baalites of long ago, they make a man their god. Shall we, then, love those who make their ruler a god?

"Whom does a true son of Israel love? Do you not recite the *Shema* every morning and evening? 'Hear, O Israel: The Lord is our God, the Lord alone. You shall love the Lord your God with all your heart, and with all your soul, and with all your might' (Deut. 6:4-5). So you see how easily a romantic mind can fall into heresy. 'Love,' indeed! But 'love the Lord your God.'

"And what is our God about in the world? God is at war against Satan. And who are under Satan's control? Those who make a god of Caesar? Yes. And those who are disobedient to God's law? Yes. Those who defile the temple? Yes. We, then, must love God but hate Satan, and make war, with God, against all those who are obedient to Satan. Right? Right!

"So now, what about those who are diseased or out of their right mind? Does our God want His people to be diseased? No. Does our God want people to lose control of their minds? No. So in whose power are these people? They are in the power of Satan or Satan's demons, are they not? Yes, to be sure!

"Here, then, comes the romantic healer. Now can a man command God? Can a man defeat Satan? No. Only God can control Satan. So the man claims to overcome Satan by healing diseases. The man claims to defeat Satan by exorcising demons from the mind. Only God can dispatch the demons. Right? So by what power does the man do these wonder works?

"Can you face the truth that shines clearly before your eyes, my young friend? Yes! The man heals diseases and exorcises demons by the power of Beelzebub, the prince of the demons, who sits on the right hand of Satan. We who are true sons of Israel, who love God with a whole heart, what are we to do with such a romantic? You know well. We must warn the disobedient Son of the error of His ways and of the danger to His soul.

"Listen carefully now, my son. If He cannot free Himself from the power of Beelzebub, what then? There are only two choices left. One, His family can commit Him to a designated cemetery for those who are proven to be demon possessed. (You only need to sign the papers and send them with me to the council.) Two, on order of the council, He must be put to death. You see, we contain the demons if possible, make war and kill the demon possessed man only if necessary."

James was stunned. He had hoped to impress the doctor with his own devotion to the law. But the doctor had not allowed him to utter a single word. He needed understanding in dealing with an agonizing family problem. He got nothing but the syllogisms of a legal mind. He wanted guidance in dealing with his brother and his mother—most of all his mother—and he got procedures for having Jesus chained in a cemetery along with the other officially certified "devils."

It was late when James lay down, but he was not to sleep well that night. Instead he would dream of cemeteries and madmen chained among the tombs, and also of demons chasing him down endless tunnels, with hideous screams reverberating all around.

At the headquarters building, oil lamps burned late into the night. The Zebedee brothers, Peter, and Simon the Zealot, huddled in a strategy meeting. Simon's informants had brought word of the arrival of a contingent of the temple police with the delegation of Jerusalem scribes. The Zebedee brothers reported on James' proposition, which they had promptly squashed. Two things worried them: the possibility that the mother of Jesus might prevail on Jesus to interrupt, or worse, to abandon the Galilee campaign; and the likelihood that the scribes were planning to make an official arrest of Jesus and take Him back to Jerusalem for trial before the council.

Plans were quickly made without consulting Jesus. Simon was dispatched to the hill country to summon Eleazar's brigands to come incognito to Capernaum, arriving with the first of the crowd that would be gathering for healings at the headquarters the next morning. Most would be stationed among the temple police, two brigands near each police officer, with orders to kill at the first show of force. Some would be posted at the doors of the headquarters and others on the roof ready to respond to any emergency on a signal from Simon, the Zealot.

While Simon hurried to the hideout of the brigands, the other disciples scattered into the night to secure weapons that could be concealed by all of Jesus' disciples so that Jesus would be protected by whichever disciples were working next to Him during the healings. They agreed not to tell Jesus of their precautions, saying to one another, "The Teacher does not need to be distracted from His healing and teaching ministry tomorrow."

Morning dawned over the Sea of Galilee like an impressionist painting both in the sky, the water, and on the beach. People gathered close to the door of the headquarters even before dawn, creating blobs of blackness on the Capernaum canvass. By the time Mary and James arrived, they could scarcely see the doorway where Jesus was healing and teaching the crowds. Just then, from behind, the trumpets of the temple police exploded in their ears, and uniformed men shoved the people to one side and the other, making way for the delegation of black-robed scribes to strut through the crowds and take up a ringside position around Jesus.

The crowds closed the passageway as quickly as it had been opened. James and Mary were at a loss as to how they would ever get close enough to make their presence known to Jesus.

"Something is wrong here," Mary said to James. "There is a feeling in the crowd that's not good."

"Uh huh." James was trying to spot one of the disciples to help them get access to Jesus.

Mary started listening to the rumors that were buzzing through the crowds. She was startled by what she heard: "The brigands have come in from the hills. They are everywhere . . . Eleazar's men . . . trouble's brewing . . . it's the temple police from Jerusalem escorting those scribes . . . the scribes are teaching . . . telling people to beware . . . trying to turn people away from Jesus . . ."

Just then some men were forcing their way out of the crowd, carrying a crippled man who was screaming in terror: "Beelzebub! He's possessed by Beelzebub! Get me out of here. The demons are tearing at me!"

As the cries of the hysterical man faded, a hush fell over the crowd. Jesus stepped up on a table, signaled for attention, and began to speak. Mary delighted in the sight of His tall and powerful stature and the resonance of His voice.

"How can Satan cast out Satan?" Jesus began.

As He spoke, it slowly dawned on Mary that Jesus was challenging the scribes and that they must have accused Him of healing in the power of Satan. "They think He is possessed!" Mary gasped, as she turned toward James, but James was not there.

Mary tuned in to Jesus' voice again as He declared: "Truly I tell you, people will be forgiven for their sins and whatever blasphemies they utter; but whoever blasphemes against the Holy Spirit can never have forgiveness, but is guilty of an eternal sin" (Mark 3:28-29). With that Jesus stepped down and went into the headquarters building.

The scribes were stunned into silence for a moment, and in that pause, a powerful voice called from the outer rim of the crowd, just behind Mary. "Jesus, your mother and brother are here! They want a word with you!"

It was Philip. Mary knew him by his voice before she could spot him, for he had been with Jesus from the beginning. Then she saw James standing with him and working his way through the crowd back to her side. The people near the doorway of the headquarters picked up the call and began shouting, "Jesus, your mother and your brothers are out here, asking for you!" Soon the whole crowd picked it up chanting: "Your mother and your brothers want you!"

The chant began to relax the tension the crowd had felt in the confrontation between Jesus and the scribes. It seemed to be defusing the violence that was brewing between the temple police and the brigands who were so well known to these Galileans.

Jesus came outdoors again, stepped up on His tabletop platform, stretched out His arms over the crowd, and called: "Who are my mother and my brothers?"

Instantly a hush fell. Mary spontaneously raised her arms toward her beloved son.

Then gesturing toward the people with their sick ones, Jesus said, "Here are my mother and my brothers! Whoever does the will of God is my brother and sister and mother" (Mark 3:34-35).

James exploded, "Those Zebedee brothers poisoned Him against us, Mother!"

Immediately, the temple police sounded their horns again, forced a passage through the crowds, heading straight toward the place where Mary and James were standing, with the scribes striding angrily behind them.

The great doctor of the law spotted James as he was leaving. He stopped, with his whole retinue, pointed his finger at James, and hissed between clenched teeth: "There you see it. Your brother refused to honor His own mother and His brothers. He is a disobedient son of Israel. And He spoke of 'sisters' in the same breath with 'brothers.' He violates the law twice in the same utterance. He is a disobedient son of Israel. It is clear for all to see. He is possessed by Beelzebub. It is punishable by death!"

The doctor whirled his robes and started off. Then he stopped and turned back to James. "You can bring those papers to me at the inn," he shouted. "We are leaving for the holy city in the morning."

Mary and James walked away from the crowd, wounded, confused, and angry. "What did the doctor mean about 'the papers,' " Mary asked, as soon as they were by themselves.

"Oh," James' mind was racing to find a cover story. He could not think of telling Mary about the cemetery option. Not now. Not yet.

"Oh, just some business I spoke with him about last night— some business for my synagogue, Mother." And then it hit James that he had dishonored his mother by his lie just as surely as Jesus had by refusing to see her. "The law is a hard taskmaster," he added, speaking only to himself.

That night, just after the moon dropped over the western horizon and the night was devoid of shadows, a knock echoed through the headquarters building. Simon, the Zealot, whose pallet lay across the doorway answered the knock—using the brigand's code. In the flickering light of a single oil lamp, the disciples drew sword and dagger and took up their assigned positions in a soundless shuffle. The silence deepened. Obviously, the brigands were not at the door, or they would have answered Simon's rap in code.

"I come alone and in peace."

"I know the voice," said Jesus. "Let him in."

Simon wedged his powerful body into the crack as he opened the door. The lamp light filtered out on to the street, and the guards on the roof signaled the "OK." A man wearing the uniform of the temple police entered the room.

"Matthias!" The name burst from Jesus' lips. But as Jesus moved to embrace him, Peter, James and John leapt forward creating a human shield against the possibility of an assassination attempt. They quickly frisked their night visitor, and Simon gave the signal to the disciples to put up their weapons.

"This is Matthias," said Jesus, with His arm around the man's shoulders as He presented him to His men. "I first met him when he was with John the Baptist." Turning to Matthias, Jesus thumped his chest on the insignia of the temple police, and added, "Perhaps you had better explain what you are doing in this uniform."

"I am the eyes and ears of the Baptizer's movement in Jerusalem. I came to show you that I will be your eyes and ears in the holy city as well. Since John was imprisoned, our cause has floundered in Judea. You, Jesus, are our best hope now. And," gesturing to the circle of men around Him, "you Galileans will need friends in Jerusalem if you are to escape the evil plots being made against you even now."

Someone pushed forward a chair for Matthias, and the group crowded around him as Simon asked, "You have a word for us then?"

"Indeed I do." Matthias turned to face Jesus as He spoke. "Your brother, James, has signed the papers to declare You a 'madman'—possessed by Satan. The scribes assure him they can get the authorization when they return to Jerusalem. They have made a deal. The scribes will drop their plans for a stoning if James can deliver on his promise to have You committed to the cemetery in Gadara." Gasps filled the room as the disciples grasped the horror of Matthias's words.

"I have been detailed to take a unit of our special forces—incognito—to Beth-yerah to arrest you as you cross the border from Galilee into Decapolis. You are to be delivered to the officers of Gadara to be chained in the cemetery there."

"When am I to be kidnapped?" Jesus asked, without a note of anxiety in His voice.

"We escort the scribes and James back to Jerusalem tomorrow. Our orders are to return with James in two weeks, arriving on the Day of Preparation. We set the ambush on the Sabbath, expecting you to leave the next day for the Feast of Tabernacles. Obviously, they are assuming that you will avoid Samaria on your way to Jerusalem as is usual for feast day pilgrims."

Jesus stood looking intently at His men. "Look at you," he said, roughing Peter's hair. "Your hand is white knuckled gripping your sword. Enough of imagining the violence that is plotted against us.

"And you, Sons of Thunder!" He was bumping James and John playfully. "Your rage has wiped out your manners.

"Matthias is one of us!" Jesus declared. "He has risked his life to come to us tonight. We have been friends a long time, and he will be with us to the end. Come, set out the bread and open the wine! Let us warm the heart of our brother before he goes out into the night."

As Jesus embraced Matthias with gratitude for his friendship, the disciples hurried into the acts of hospitality, talking furiously about the disclosures Matthias had made. Simon, then, took command again; he ordered all the lamps snuffed out and saw Matthias out of the door without danger of detection.

Jesus lit again the oil lamp and addressed His men: "Back to your pallets, men, and sleep well with what is left of the night. Tomorrow, make ready the boat while I am at work with the crowds who are awaiting us here. For tomorrow evening we cross the sea to Beth-yerah. From there we go to Gadara. 'Madmen' in the cemetery there need us."

Comments on Story: A Night Visitor

The Action

One of the ways to allow a story like "A Night Visitor" to speak to you is to ask yourself, "What in me is most like the various parts of the story?" Reflecting on the action of the story, the most obvious is that James and Mary are trying to save Jesus from a heretic's death. As you launch into the Christian adventure in your own life, what is it in you that wants to save Jesus from criticism, misunderstanding, and rejection? What do you tend to do in such times? Are you tempted to confuse your love for Jesus with your needs to resist change, to serve your own ambitions for advancement in the eyes of other Christians, or to be loyal to the beliefs and forms of worship in which you were reared as if they were the last word, absolutely beyond error in all times and places?

You may wish to put the book down at this point and linger over these questions. Some people find it helpful to write out thoughts that come to mind while doing self-examination of this kind. At each set of thought questions that follow, you may repeat the process of personal reflection.

James and Mary were defeated in their efforts to save Jesus from His enemies by the interplay of many vectors of force— forces that preceded their family crisis, forces that exceeded their own sphere of influence, and forces that have the marks of divine Providence breaking into human affairs. We do well to reflect on the jet streams of our society that determine the specific events we must cope with from day to day.

Using the story as a pattern, one of the social forces in Jesus' day was that of the wilderness communities. Both John the Baptist and Jesus were nourished in this context prior to their public ministries. Both reacted against the wilderness way and moved beyond their starting places as they matured spiritually.

Remember that the wilderness groups were religiously serious, rigidly bound by hundreds of rules and regulations, and strictly separated from the mainstream of society. They believed dogmatically in their own religious superiority, their favorite status as God's chosen ones, and the fantasy that God would deliver them from their enemies and make them rulers over all if they would only keep the rules perfectly.

Pause for reflection as to what in your experience may be similar. Have you moved beyond your point of entry into the Christian adventure? If so, what prompted you? In what direction have you moved? Are you open to allowing your choices to be challenged by the story of Jesus?

Another jet-stream pattern governing the weather of Jesus' world was the movement led by John the Baptist. John broke with his wilderness community by requiring absolute honesty in one's dealings with others, justice for the "little people" of the society, and an inclusive, welcoming attitude toward all who truly repented and submitted to inner cleansing of their attitudes and actions. He required a radical change of heart and of behavior. Baptism was a public confession by the Jews that they were no better in God's eyes than the Gentiles. They were making a fresh start as adults on their spiritual journey.

Now ask yourself, "When and where in my world of experience have I opted for absolute honesty, moral integrity, and done so in a serious way? Have I, like John the Baptist, been harsh and condemning of those who have not come to repentance as I have? Have I felt superior to others and expected God to reward me in dramatic and highly visible ways for my religious zeal? (Pause for reflection as to what in your experience may be similar.)

Then there were the scribes, the doctors of the law, and also the Sadducees and Pharisees. All of these groups supported the traditional religious institutions and the most conservative interpretations of the law and of temple worship. The Sadducees were the more affluent and politically powerful of these groups. The Pharisees were the leaders of the rank and file of the people. Scribes were the learned specialists in Scripture and tradition. They had many differences among themselves, but they had some things in common. They supported "law and order" as the ultimate good for the country. They believed that their interpretations of Scripture were the only interpretations possible. They reasoned that, as defenders of conventional religion, they had the right to put to death anyone who held different views or proposed changes that would upset the status quo.

In short, the religious leaders of the day lived on the basis that the end justifies the means. Thus, because Jesus was violating their rules and threatening their hold on the reins of power, they felt they could use any weapon to destroy Him. They could vilify Him to the people, accusing Him of healing in the power of Beelzebub. They could have Him committed to a living death, chained in a cemetery. They could stone Him to death or conspire to have the Roman government crucify Him. Also they could bribe the guards at the tomb to spread the lie that His disciples stole His body from the grave in order to discredit reports of His resurrection.

So ask yourself, now, what part of you is tempted to use any means to maintain the status quo in your world of experience When and under what circumstances are you likely to spread gossip or embellish the facts about someone in order to discredit them in the eyes of others? When and toward whom do you become cruel? Or cutting? Irrationally angry? In what groups do you tend to join others in character assassination? Have you found that participation in some churches stimulates your passion to condemn, attack, and punish people who are different? Does your loyalty to a political party or a cause tempt you to accept smear tactics in the media designed to destroy your opponents? Does the appeal to "law and order" ease your conscience about such tactics? Does the appeal to wage "holy war" against the enemies of God make you feel religiously superior to your opponents—like God's "chosen" people? (Pause for reflection as to what in your experience may be similar.)

Another set of forces was working in the story. A cluster of factors shaped the disciples of Jesus and led to the appearance, at the end of the story, of Matthias, a "secret disciple" serving in the forces of the temple police. The disciples were mainly Galileans. They grew up in the north of Palestine, far from the center of power in Jerusalem. They were a rough and ready group of working people. They were fiercely independent in spirit, living on the margins of economic survival for the most part.

The brigands who survived in the hills were a mixed group of people wanted for crimes they had committed or seeking revenge of those who had violated them or their families. Some were political freedom fighters opposing Roman rule. Others were desperadoes wanted for raiding property and killing hated members of the Jewish gentry. Wealthy Jews who collaborated with the Romans or with Herod, the puppet governor of the region, were their victims as well. The brigands enjoyed the protection of the common people of Galilee, all of whom suffered under the excessive taxation and economic exploitation of governmental and military institutions.

Rabbis in Galilee were identified with the people more than with the ruling classes. They tended to oppose the oppressive rules of Jerusalem-based Judaism. Jesus described the common people as "sheep without a shepherd" and found Galileans responsive to His vision of the kingdom of God and to His works of compassion among them.

In reflection on your own adventure in living, ask yourself when and where you may have met people or been a part of a group who were not highly educated, not power hungry, and perhaps not active in organized religion, but who were down to earth, honest about themselves, and thought clearly about the difference between what is decent and indecent in human relationships. What is the part of you that responds positively to such simplicity and honesty about life? What is the part of you that sides with the poor and powerless against the rich and mighty?

At the same time you may be aware of a part of you that is threatened by social activists, especially when they support

open conflict between social classes, conduct protest demonstrations, strikes, or rallies that inspire hatred and violence.
What does the story show you as an alternative to the brigands
on one hand and the scribes with their police forces on the
other?

Have you experienced the difference a group can make in
whether or not your integrity and generosity toward yourself
and others tends to flower or wilt? What kinds of groups help
you to be compassionate, to be in touch with your common
sense, and to give yourself wholeheartedly to the people and
causes that serve unselfishly the needs of others? (Pause for reflection as to what in your experience may be similar.)

The Characters

Now that you have reflected on yourself and your loyalties
among the many social movements and power groups in society, you may gain further insight into yourself by asking what
part of you is most like the characters in the story.

James, the brother of Jesus, was loyal to his family and the
faith of his ancestors. He was genuinely concerned to save Jesus
from a heretic's death. His motives were mixed with his career
ambitions as a student of the law in Jerusalem. He was not a
disciple of Jesus at this point in the story. (After Jesus' death he
was to become a Christian and the leader of the Jerusalem
church.) At this time, James was most sympathetic to the cause
of John the Baptist. He wanted all people to become strict ob-
servers of the law, but he wanted nothing to do with the spiritual freedom that Jesus displayed in His healing and caring
ministries.

So what is the part of you that prefers to be true to the conventional religion of your rearing without asking any hard questions? When do you find yourself responding to deeply troubled
people by talking about religious rules rather than listening well
and trying to understand the inner pain and longings of the other person? Do you find that your seriousness about your faith

keeps you from responding to life in spontaneous, childlike joyfulness? When push comes to shove in your life, do you find that you tend to rely on the authorities who put tradition above compassion, keeping the letter of the law above discerning and trusting the spirit of the law?

These are the parts of you that are most like James, the brother of Jesus. What do you admire most in yourself when you are like James? What are your strengths? What qualities would you not want to lose if you were to join the band of Jesus' disciples in the story? What are your limitations? What is missing in your life when you are locked into the James way of being? What is it about James that makes it impossible for him to be a disciple of Jesus at this point in his life? What would have to change were he to become a disciple?

Mary, like most women in Jesus' day, would not have received any formal education. She began childbearing at age twelve or thirteen, and her life was devoted in the main to managing the family and rearing her children. She had virtually no legal rights and no access to the public issues of the day. She was wise in the realities of life, however, loyal to her loves, and true to her vision of Jesus as a prophet.

It was Mary's initiative that launched Jesus' public ministry in Galilee at the wedding in Cana. Her bond with Jesus was so strong that she could not refuse James' pressure to go with him to try to save Jesus from the heretic's death He was inviting by His open violation of the law. Her loyalty to Jesus transcended her fears, however. She followed Jesus to Jerusalem for the Passover during which Jesus was crucified. She was among the women at the foot of the cross, and she continued into her old age to be a faithful part of the early Christian community in Jerusalem. (Now pause for reflection as to what in your experience may be similar.)

What is the part of you that is most like Mary in putting the people who matter to you above causes and crusades? Do you, like Mary, value positive relationships more than personal power and influence in society? Are you content to work quietly

behind the scenes to promote the careers of loved ones who
have leadership abilities? What kind of sticking power do you
have in staying with a person who is in big trouble to the bitter
end? What are the rewards of being like Mary in these ways?
What are the limits?

Consider next the Galilean disciples. Simon the Zealot;
James and John, the sons of Zebedee (also called Sons of Thunder); and Peter appear in the story before us. All four of them
were aggressive and prone to violence in coping with a crisis.
The Zealots were committed to the violent overthrow of the
Roman rulers. The sons of Zebedee wanted to call down fire on
the Samaritan city that would not receive them (Luke 9:51-56).
Peter drew his sword and attacked the temple police as they
were arresting Jesus in the garden of Gethsemane. The Zebedee
brothers were aggressive in advancing their own careers at the
expense of the harmony and morale of the other ten disciples, as
we see in the account of their seeking the top positions in Jesus'
kingdom (Mark 10:35-41).

In the story "A Night Visitor," we see these disciples coping
with the threat from the Jerusalem scribes in their characteris-
tic way. They form an alliance with the brigands of the district;
they arm the entire group of disciples; and they form a military
shield around Jesus without bringing Him into their strategy.
They reject James's proposal out of hand and presumably influence Jesus to reject the appeal to receive His mother and brother, James, under the circumstances. Then, out of the night,
comes Matthias, a spy in the ranks of the temple police, with
information that saves Jesus from a secret arrest when he
crossed from Galilee into Decapolis. (We learn in Acts 1:21-26
that Matthias was one of those who were loyal to Jesus from His
baptism to His ascension. Matthias was chosen to replace Judas
among the twelve.)

Reflecting on these characters, ask yourself about the part of
you that responds to life by aggressively attacking problems.
What connections do you feel as you see these men protecting
themselves and their Master with the weapons of combat and of

destruction? Do you sense an inner kinship with them in their regional pride, their rural origins, and their resentment of officials who try to impose their religious authority and power on them from outside of their region of the country?

The villains in the story, as in the biblical record, are the scribes who pursue Jesus up to Galilee to discredit Him, to get evidence of heresy, and if possible, to arrest Him and take Him back to Jerusalem for trial and death by stoning. We need to be careful in reading the Gospels not to read references to "the Jews" who sought Jesus' death as a condemnation of all Jews then and now. Anti-Semitism has hidden behind the Jesus story far too long. It has no support in an accurate reading of Christian beginnings. We would have no Christian story at all if it had not been for "the Jews." Not only was Jesus a Jew reared in a Jewish family and a Jewish world, but also His followers were Jews. All of His disciples were from "the Jews." With only a few exceptions, Jesus limited His ministry to "the Jews." For years after Jesus' death and resurrection, all of the members of the mother church were from "the Jews." The great missionaries to the Gentiles were outstanding Jews: Peter, Saul who became Paul, Barnabas who sponsored Paul and accompanied him, and many others. "The Jews" in the providence of God provided not only the legacy out of which the Christ could come and within which the mystery of incarnation can be discerned, but also the bodies and the minds, the hearts and the sacrifices by which the story survived and was spread worldwide.

There is a more personal reason for not making "the Jews" a racial scapegoat. That will come clear as you ask yourself the question: What is the part of me that is most like the scribes in the story before us? Begin by looking for the part of you that wishes the worst for those who upset you or oppose you. Try to be open to your desires for revenge, for getting even, for shutting up and getting rid of those who make you mad. Check out the possibility that you privately feel superior to others in your family or that your family is of superior stock to your in-laws or neighbors.

A basic flaw in the scribes was their assumption that God's last word had been spoken in the Old Testament. They also felt they were the sole possessors of the truth of their sacred Scriptures. They had no awareness of the way God continues to speak to people from generation to generation. They also felt that they were duty bound to protect God's Word from all challenges. In doing so, they used any method to silence questions and to protect their traditional ways of thinking.

What is the part of you that would like to believe that you are part of a tradition that has the last word on every aspect of God's will? Can you sense a readiness to believe that no one is doing God's work in the world as well as you or those who believe as you do? Do you feel obligated to fight and if possible destroy those who serve God in different ways, those who disagree with your group on important beliefs? Something of the scribes lives in everyone. We do well to see these attitudes in ourselves and in our own faith group and to seek to be delivered from them rather than to blame others and to make scapegoats of different faith groups than our own. (Now pause for reflection as to what in your experience may be similar.)

The Theme

The themes of the story are implicit in the questions for reflection in the preceding paragraphs. One theme stands out above the others, however. The key word is *beyond.*

John the Baptist went beyond the wilderness community and its influence on his faith experience. Jesus went beyond John the Baptist's movement. Jesus also went beyond loyalty to His family in saying "Whoever does the will of God is my brother and sister and mother." Looking past the story of "A Night Visitor," we see the disciples at Pentecost being awakened to an experience of Jesus as Holy Spirit that went beyond their experience of Him in the flesh. Then, in the years after Pentecost, the apostles were forced by Peter's experience in the home of a

Gentile, Cornelius, to go beyond their narrow view of God's chosen people, to a universal view—to see God acting to choose Gentiles as well as Jews and thereby to make it clear that all peoples everywhere are the chosen people of God.

The Christian adventure is not completed in a single step. The first step is a point of no return, but it only begins the adventure. The Christian adventure is a journey beyond the point of no return. A pilgrim is awakened again and again and again to the presence of God. Faith is always taking the next step, but the next step is never the last step on the journey.

Why do some people welcome the adventure of faith and others take root after the first step and refuse to go beyond? The Gospels give us only two pictures of Jesus' childhood, but both hold clues useful in rearing children who will be ready for the Christian adventure. The first is the flight into Egypt. Joseph was warned in a dream, "Get up, take the child and his mother, and flee to Egypt, and remain there until I tell you; for Herod is about to search for the child, to destroy him" (Matt. 2:13). The second is Jesus in the temple at age twelve.

Parents do well to be sensitive to the environment in which they rear their children. Power hungry, evil-spirited adults pose great dangers to the spiritual growth of children. A church suffering from chronic conflict is an evil and destructive environment for children. Communities that tolerate prejudice and scapegoating in their schools and churches are hazardous for the spiritual health of children and youth. To ignore the lethal traffic in drugs and alcohol among youth is like ignoring radioactive emissions from a nearby nuclear reactor. Parents who encourage preoccupation with status in dress codes and social activities and school officials who violate regulations in order to produce winning teams in athletic events undermine the spiritual health of the children in their charge. At times a family may need to uproot itself and take drastic steps to protect the children from social systems and institutions, including churches at times, when these systems are filled with an evil spirit.

More common and often more dangerous to children's spiritual health, however, is the marriage and kinship system in which chronic conflict stifles spiritual awareness. Emotional or physical abuse creates images of a God who seems cruel, capricious, or indifferent if not totally absent to the child trapped in psychic pain. A whole family may need to "Get up, take the child" and "flee" not to Egypt, but to a good (preferably Christian) family therapist who can help the family escape the destructive power of their own family system gone bad.

The second picture we have of Jesus in His youth occurred as He crossed the threshold into full membership in the household of faith. The context for the story in this chapter began with the account of Jesus "listening to [the teachers in the temple] and asking them questions" (Luke 2:41-51). As noted in the previous comments, Jesus was identifying with the faith of His family and of His Jewish culture. At the same time, Jesus was questioning His tradition.

An important difference between Christian education for youth that stifles spiritual growth and that which stimulates and frees spiritual growth is at the point of questioning one's tradition. Youth ministries that support the questioning of one's tradition while guiding in the Scriptural examination of that tradition may be upsetting to some parents. Jesus' parents were upset that He was not dutifully in place with them as they returned from the Passover. Jesus, however, had the inner strength to begin to separate Himself from His family of origin as He was identifying Himself with His family of faith. The Christian adventure calls for parents who understand and provide for their children resources in the church that support the questioning process as an essential part of a young person's own spiritual journey.

A third and final note on preparing youth to welcome the adventure of Christian living is sounded in Jesus' wilderness temptations. The context of the story shows that Jesus' temptations involved wrestling with the prevailing options within the religious movements of His time. Baptism had already taken place. In baptism Jesus crossed the point of no return. He took His stand with those who honored the Hebrew Scripture and sought to integrate their faith and their way of life in obedience to God. The temptations came after Jesus' public commitment. And so it has been for many people ever since. It is only after taking a stand within a particular faith community and surrendering to live in obedience to God that you realize how many different ways there are for living out your newly chosen faith.

As with Jesus, so with us. One option is to reinvent the wheel of religious community. Turning stones into bread would have made Jesus a second Moses. Jesus chose to stay within the Mosaic tradition, however. He went for the heart, for wholehearted love of God and neighbor, no matter what institutional structure one had inherited.

Going for the kingdoms of the world would have made Jesus a political messiah and Jerusalem the capital of a world empire. Jesus chose instead a Kingdom "not from this world" (John 18:36), instructing His disciples to turn the other cheek and go the second mile when coerced by legal and military powers. He invested His hopes in the power of love rather than the power of force and violence. He created a community of mutual care rather than of hierarchy, chain of command, and secret strategy sessions.

From the pinnacle of the temple, Jesus had the opportunity to leap into history as the highest of all the high priests in all of the world's religions. He could have combined the best of the Mosaic law, the prophets' passion for justice, and a wisdom beyond that of all the sages of humankind. He could have done so within the structure of the temple in Jerusalem. Instead, He chose to venture down a road that led Him to be judged a heretic, misunderstood by His family to be a madman, and then to die a criminal's death, judged a traitor to His country. Before going public, Jesus set His priority on the truth that sets us free—free from the tyranny of temples, free from the pretensions of prophecy, and free from the self-deceptions of a cut-flower spirituality.

As we follow the public ministry of Jesus in the chapters that follow, we shall try to enter the joy and the suffering that flow from the choices that Jesus made when He dared to go beyond the initial point of no return. Perhaps in reading on, you will experience a growing excitement about the Christian adventure and decide to reorder your priorities in order to step beyond the point at which you made your initial commitment to the Jesus story.

Notes

1. Raymond E. Brown, *New Testament Essays* (New York: Paulist Press, 1965).

4

In the Presence

Conflict storms through every marker event in the Jesus story. Conflict was a major theme in Mary's response to her pregnancy. She sang of God scattering the proud, putting down the mighty from their thrones, and sending the rich away empty. Conflict wore the evil face of Herod, ordering the slaughter of every male child in Bethlehem under two years of age. The conflicts of youth against their parents and of questions beating against tradition were the backdrop for Jesus' entrance into manhood, as He chose to remain in the temple ("my Father's house") questioning the teachers rather than to go home with His parents on schedule. Conflict grew fierce after His baptism, in the wilderness temptations. Coming off His victory over the tempter, Jesus entered His public ministry, only to find Himself in the eye of a hurricane of conflicting needs, beliefs, and passions every step of the way leading to His crucifixion.

Ironically, Jesus was in conflict not only with those who gave absolute authority to their interpretation of the Torah, but also with His own disciples. He struggled against their blindness, trying to help them see evidence of the unseen world breaking through into the everyday, see-touch world. Jesus wanted them to see that God was at work healing, forgiving, teaching, casting out unclean spirits, enjoying party times, calming storms, and feeding them—at all times, not just in the miracle moments. God was leading them and feeding them now just as God did for their forebears under Moses in the wilderness. Jesus was moving heaven and earth, almost literally, trying to waken the people's desire for God.

Jesus wanted to stretch their minds to see that God was not limited at any time, not even by Sabbath laws. He struggled to help them see that the kingdom of God was a spiritual and not a political kingdom. His message was that "the kingdom of God has come near" (Mark 1:15). He longed for His closest followers to wake up and see that the kingdom of God was really good news. But He knew people had to turn away from their old ways of seeing things and to believe the good news before they would be able to see it.

Most people agree with the saying, "Seeing is believing." Jesus struggled to get His followers to discover that "believing is seeing." The crowds saw Jesus perform miracle after miracle, but many did not believe that He was God's anointed, the Christ, the Son of God. Not until they began to believe that Jesus was the Christ would they begin to see what He was really about when, for example, He blessed five loaves and two fish and with them served thousands of people who had spent the day at His feet hearing His vision of the kingdom of God on earth.

One of the events that captures Jesus' struggle to open the eyes of His own disciples (an event reported in each of the four Gospels) is the feeding of the thousands. Mark was the first to write of this event, and he gave a key for understanding the story and the discussion that follows.

Mark wrote his version of the life of Jesus to show the church of his day that Jesus revealed the secret of His being the Christ, the Son of God, in what He did. The Gospel of Mark is a book of action. The word *immediately* ties one event to another, over and over again. Here, as well, the staccato beat goes on. After the disciples "took up twelve baskets full of broken pieces and of the fish," the passage reads, "Immediately he made his disciples get into the boat and go on ahead to the other side, to Bethsaida, while he dismissed the crowd." Jesus then went into the hills to pray. About the fourth watch of the night He saw that

His disciples were in trouble: "they were straining at the oars against an adverse wind." So "he came towards them early in the morning, walking on the sea." They were "terrified." Jesus calmed their fears, "and the wind ceased." The final sentence of Mark's account reads: "And they were utterly astounded, for they did not understand about the loaves"; and in *The Good News Bible* the final word is: "Their minds could not grasp it" (Mark 6:45-52).

Jesus' struggle with His disciples' blindness comes sharply into focus in the words, "They had not understood the real meaning of the feeding of the five thousand; their minds could not grasp it" (GNB). In spite of all the healings, teachings, and miracles of raising the dead and feeding thousands with no more than a sack lunch, the disciples could not get it through their heads. They were "seeing but not believing."

How, then, did Jesus work with this block in the minds of His own disciples? What would it take for reasonable people to "grasp it"—to "understand about the loaves"? These are the questions that prompt the story of Michael, a ten-year-old boy as he himself tells it.

Imagine Michael as a student in a Hebrew school responding to an assignment by the rabbi to write a story on the topic: "A Day I Will Long Remember." Michael lived in a small village a few miles from the Sea of Galilee. The story has been "translated" into English with an attempt to keep the flavor of the elementary level of education in the underdeveloped area of Galilee where Michael lived.[1]

Story: A Day at the Lake

Ma said I could go fishin' last time we have a school holiday. She say, "A boy can git closer to God out by the lake than sittin' in a dark, stuffy synagogue school." Which sounds reasonable.

I waked up before the birds begin to sing. I moved quiet as a mouse so as not to wake Ma. She'd laid out a barley loaf and a salt-cured fish fer my lunch. But I know'd she had plenty more 'cause she was at the village oven all day. So I kind of stuffed my lunch sack full. There was maybe six or seven loaves and quite a few fishes, too. "I gotta feed Miz all day today," I says to myself. (Miz is my dog. I named him Mizpah on account of that's the name of the watchtower over by the lake, and Miz is my watchtower.) It took one fish just to keep Miz quiet so's he wouldn't wake Ma while we was gettin' the fishin' gear ready.

Miz know'd where we was goin', soon as he seen me reach fer my tackle box. We dug worms and was gone, Miz runnin' out ahead. I were as excited as Miz. Soon as we was out of earshot of the house, I started whistlin' right along with the birds, which was wakin' up. There ain't nothin' purtier than the sky when the sun's a wakin' up. Comin' down on the lake from the nor'west as we do, the hills on the east is dark as a cave, with the sky shootin' light rays all'round 'em. I 'member thinking, "Sure is a mysterious place, this here Sea of Galilee."

Fishin' were no good that mornin' a'tall. Wind out o' the north were the problem. I were feelin' bad about not catchin' anything. Really wanted to take Ma a good catch, so she'd maybe fergit about me takin' so many loaves and all. One thing sure: I weren't "gittin' close to God" like Ma said. Thinkin' 'bout that made me right mad. I says to myself, "if God wanted to git close to me, you'd think He would send some fish my way." It made me wonder, too, if maybe our Rebbe was right 'bout God comin' to us in the law 'stead of in nature, which is what the Baalites say. [Editor's note: Rebbe is pronounced with a long *e*. It is the correct Hebrew pronunciation for the term for Rabbi.]

I didn't have time to do much thinkin' on it, though. Right then Miz set out barkin' up a storm. I saw dust risin' over the hill. Must o' been thousands of people walkin'—no, more like runnin'—my way. I'd never saw so many people in one place afore in my whole life. They was headed right fer the beach where I were campin' out.

I were so scared seein' this herd o' people stampedin' on me I dropped my fishin' rod and dove into the bushes to hide. Fast as Miz could run, they was on my beach, ever'where. Some of 'em was plum crazy, even sloshing out into the water. They was

pointin' and shouting, "Here they come! Headin' this way!"
And sure 'nuf, there was a fishin' boat, the men pulling at the
oars, headin' in. Soon as they beached her, the crowd started
up, like a pack o' yelpin' hounds, shoutin' questions at this Rebbe who was movin' to the front of the boat. They was all worked
up about politicians and taxes and what God were goin'a do
'bout it.

Well, that Rebbe raised His hands over 'em, and they quiet'd
down like givin' suck to a squalin' baby. Then it hit me. I'd left
my lunch sack out there in the middle of that crowd, as well as
my fishin' gear. I know'd fishin' were done for the day, but I
sure hated the thought o' losin' my lunch. So while ever'one was
fixin' their eyes on the Rebbe who were gittin' out of the boat, I
slunked out among 'em to git my sack. Just as I grabbed it and
looked up to see which way to run, there was the Rebbe standin'
over me.

His eyes—hit were His eyes had a holt o' me, not the hand
which he put on my head. I were quiverin' like a rabbit sensin'
danger. Then the Rebbe said som'thin' 'bout "sheep without a
shepherd," and the quiverin' went away. I felt warm and safe all
over, like Ma a tuckin' me in at bedtime.

I know'd right then I weren't goin' to run away. I were fixin'
to stay as close to the Rebbe as I could. Well, He got that crowd
up the hill a piece and settled down, found Hisself a rock to sit
on and started teachin'. It hit me right then: the Rebbe done
turned this lakeside into a synagogue school, only it weren't
dark and stuffy like at home.

Well, most of the Rebbe's teachin's was about the kingdom o'
God. I don't pay much attention to politics talk, myself. Ma
always says to me, "Michael, don't you never get mixed up in
politics. Politics," she say, "is like a snake in the rocks. Let it
bite you, and all you git is all swelled up or killed, one." So I
figur' this Rebbe is another one of them messiah-type fellers
that are bound to git hauled off to Jerusalem and nailed up on a
tree to die.

I perked up my ears, though, when the Rebbe say, "You all

are God's people when others call you names on account o' Me." Right then, I thunk about Josh, at school, a callin' me names 'cause I ain't got a pa. And then the Rebbe say, "When that happens to you, be cheerful 'cause you have a Heavenly Father. And He loves you."

I thunk that over fer quite a spell. Next time Josh call me that name, I'll jes tell him, "I does too have a pa. My Pa's in heaven, and He love me better'n your ol' man who's drunk most o' the time."

'Bout then the Rebbe were gettin' after those folks pretty good. He say, "You all are like kids playing in the streets and shouting at each other, 'We put on fast music fer dancing, but you wouldn't dance; so we put on slow music fer wailin', but you wouldn't go into mournin'. Fer John (the one what were baptizin' folks) offered a hard life, and you people say, 'John is looney.' I offer laughter and joy, and you say, 'Look at him. He's a bum who runs around with the wrong crowd, partyin' and drinkin'.' So, if *intelligence* can be judged by its fruits, well!" The Rebbe got a good laugh on 'em that time. Lot o' folks were belly laughin', but some o' them religious fellers was looking sour as if they had just et a persimmon.

I sure wished Ma were there when the Rebbe got to talking' 'bout worry. He says, "God's people don't worry about stuff all the time, like what you'll eat or what you'll wear." Then he says the funniest thing: "Take a look at the birds. They don't plant or harvest; they don't store things away in storehouses. Yet God takes care of them. You are a heap more valuable than birds." And from birds in general he goes to sparrows. "Not a single sparrow falls to the ground without your Heavenly Father knowin' 'bout it. Why even the hairs of your head is numbered. So don't be scared and worry all the time. You is worth more than a lot of sparrows."

I think about that, ever' time I sees a bird or combs my hair.

Someone in the crowd hollered out askin' the Rebbe 'bout what happened when they was in Gadara the other day. And He told the spookiest story I ever heard. Seems they was a goin' there to help some crazy people. I never know'd afore that crazies was chained in cemeteries, but that's what they do in Gadara anyhow. Well, this one man never wore no clothes. A lot o' times he done broke his chains. The demons in him run him out into the desert sometimes too. Well, when the Rebbe show up, that crazy man start yellin' at the top o' his lungs, "What you got against me, God's holy boy? I warns you, don't you put the screws on me!"

The Rebbe ask him, "What's your name?"

He say, "Multitude," since a slew of demons was in him.

Then the demons start beggin' Him not to send 'em into exile, but to let 'em go into a herd of hogs there on the hillside. When they does, the whole herd goes tearing down the slope into the lake and drowns.

News o' that spreads like fire and soon the whole town were runnin' to the cemetery. There the man were, sittin' at the Rebbe's feet, fully clothed and completely sane.

Well, it scares the daylight out o' them folks. They was shakin' like crazy. They begs the Rebbe and His helper fellers to leave 'em be, so that's that. They gets in their boat and comes back to Capernaum.

This kingdom o' God that the Rebbe keep talkin' 'bout makes a lot o' sense to me. He takes in even the crazies and makes 'em right in the head, and He don't blink an eye at losing a whole herd o' hogs to do it. What I can't figur' out is why those people in Gadara run the Rebbe off after He done such a wonderful thing.

Later on the Rebbe told us a story that made me feel real special! Hit was 'bout this man who had a hundred sheep, and a little lamb got lost. So he leaves the ninety-nine and hunts for the lost lamb. When he finds it, he puts it on his shoulders and goes home with it. Well, he's bubblin' with joy, so he calls to his neighbors, "Hey, y'all, come on over. I'm givin' a party to celebrate findin' my little lost lamb."

Then, the Rebbe say, "I'm atellin' you, there'll be more joy in the kingdom o' God over one little 'outsider' who gets brought into the fold than over the ninety-nine religious people who just hang around in the old pastures and never know what hit's like to be out there all alone and lost and then to get found and loved by the good shepherd."

I was feelin' just like that little lamb while He was telling the story. Ain't nobody in synagogue ever noticed me, or put a arm around me like a real friend.

Next thing I know'd, He was alayin' it on the super religious types. Called 'em "phonies": how they make a big deal of praying in public; how they put on long faces and act like big shots in the synagogue. He say that prayin's just talkin' to our Heavenly Father, and bein' fer Him and His kingdom, and then askin' fer what we need to be kingdom-type folks.

I been praying like that ever since, myself. Hits funny how many things just kind o' work out good lately.

There was one thing the Rebbe say that I'm still not sure 'bout, though. He was sayin' that when some bully takes your stuff, you should let him have it. If he makes you give him your shirt, you should give him your undershirt too. Then He say, "Love your enemies, and you'll be the spittin' image o' God. 'Cause God is kind and friendly even toward people that are ugly and mean."

I don't know if I can live that way, but when the Rebbe's talkin', I get to feelin' like I could, sure 'nuf.

There were som'thin' else 'bout the Rebbe I couldn't believe, even though I keep seeing it happen. It were the way He made ever'one feel good 'bout the'selves. He never made nobody feel stupid or ashame' for not knowin' som'thin' or bein' wrong 'bout it, which our Rebbe at school does ever day. He never once hit out with a mad voice, not even when some of the religious fellers got uppity and tried to put Him down. And His voice: His voice came from the middle 'o the earth; it had the beat o' the waves on the shore, and the music in it of a breeze in the cedar trees. He might near put me into a trance, just a listenin' to the sound.

Next thing I know'd, the day-endin' shadows was crawling

right up the hill into the crowd. The men that was travelin' with the Rebbe had Him hid in the middle of 'em. They was talkin' all 'citedlike 'bout som'thin'. One of 'em shouted, "It would take a whole year's wages, it would!" The Rebbe's voice calmed him down right quick, though. Then those helper fellers scattered out all over the hillside, shoutin' at people and gittin' 'em split into groups, and sayin', "The Master say, 'we're goin' to break bread together afore we part."

All of a sudden, one of them fellers were squattin' down aside o' me. "My name is Andrew," he say, "what's your name, young man?"

"Michael," I mumbles. I figur' he was up to som'thin', but he seem 'bout as nice as the Rebbe.

"Michael, I've noticed how still you've been, sitting here listenin' to the Teacher all afternoon. And I was right next to you on the beach when we got here. I saw the Master lay His hand on you and bless you. I knew you were just trying to save your lunch from this crowd, but when you followed the Master up the hill and forgot about your tackle box and fishing pole, I just felt that something special was happening in your heart—maybe a bond of love with the Teacher? Am I right?" I were dumb struck. I opened my mouth and couldn't git out a word. Then he says, "And Michael, I picked up your fishin' gear and put it in our boat where it would be safe. So be sure to let me get it for you before you go home."

"Gee, thanks!" I says in a whisper.

"And Michael," he goes on, "the Teacher is askin' folks to give Him any food they may have with 'em, so that He can feed ever'one who is here before they go home. Would you let Him have your lunch sack too?"

I tell you, that Andrew feller had me right there. I'd a give Him my fishin' stuff and maybe even old Miz if he'd a asked. So I hands over my lunch sack, which still had five loaves and two fishes left in it. But I admit that he hadn't took two steps away before I begun to wonder if I hadn't just been suckered out o' what was left, and why I hadn't been smart enough to eat it during the afternoon, 'stead of sittin' there in a trance listenin' to the Rebbe.

Next thing I knew, them helper fellers was huddled 'round the Rebbe again. When the Rebbe come out of that huddle, He held up my sack and said in a big voice: "We have five barley loaves and two fish, thanks to young Michael, sittin' here at my feet."

I suppose He went on into the Blessing fer the food then, but I didn't hear another word. I felt as big as the mountain and wanted to hide in the bottom of the sea, all at the same time. The Rebbe knew my name. And He was blessing Ma's fixins, which I had gotten that mornin'.

I was mixed up 'bout that. I hadn't felt good all day about stuffin' my sack with that extra food, but if I hadn't of, I sure wouldn't have had a thing left over for Mr. Andrew and the Rebbe. By time I come to my senses again and noticed what was goin' on, I seed that ever'one—thousands of 'em—was eating as much as they wanted, and them helper fellers was goin' round with baskets pickin' up the leftovers.

After that the crowd just kinda melted into the shadows of the day's dyin'. Mr. Andrew were true to his word. He git my fishin' stuff fer me and seed to it that I et my supper out o' those baskets o' leftovers too. Then Miz and I headed home. It got dark on us afore we got there, but Miz know'd the way, and I weren't a bit scared. I didn't even worry about the whippin' Ma were likely to give me for takin all that food.

Truth to tell, I haven't worried about hardly anythin' since that day. Somehow, I just know'd that God was on that hillside.

And He know my name.

Comments on Story: A Day at the Lake

You may want to give yourself a few minutes to befriend the story, that is, to think about it in an easy kind of way. You might like to recall the scenes that stand out in your memory or remember what came to your mind at those points in the story.

Then ask yourself: Were there any surprises in the story?

Usually when a person pays attention to the surprises, they open some doors into a fuller understanding of the story as a whole.

For me, the big surprise was realizing that Michael never once puzzled over the miracle involved in feeding that crowd with just his sack lunch of five loaves and two fish. What captured Michael's mind was that the rabbi knew his name. That leads me to see that it was Jesus Himself who held Michael's attention from the moment they first met on the beach. Michael was scared, but at Jesus' touch he felt warm and safe. Michael thought of Jesus as another rabbi, like his teacher at school, but this one was different. He did not put people down, and His voice had a quality Michael had never experienced before. Looking back on "A Day I Will Long Remember," Michael said, "Somehow, I just know'd that God was on that hillside. And He know my name."

Michael, unlike the disciples, did understand about the loaves. Michael got the message that the "helper fellers" missed. His mind got the secret: Jesus is the Son of God. But Michael grasped the secret because he experienced Jesus, not because he saw a miracle. He experienced a miracle that the others missed. He gave himself to the miraculous spirit of the rabbi.

This, then, is what it means to say "believing is seeing." The Spirit awakened Michael to the presence of God there at the seaside. He believed that in Jesus he had been met by God. He experienced the *desire for God*. Therefore, he could see and "understand about the loaves." Of course, Jesus could make a boy's lunch serve thousands. God was there breaking the loaves and providing plenty for all. That's how God is—generous! extravagant! loving everyone alike!

One further word about Michael: he was not political. His mind had not closed on the conviction that God just had to save His people politically. Michael was aware of "them messiah-type fellers," of which there were hundreds in the time of Roman rule. Surely, like every Jewish boy, Michael had heard the

rabbis talk of a coming messiah who would deliver them because they were God's chosen people. The main difference between Michael and the disciples might well have been that the
boy did not have to unlearn the selfish, earthbound adult ideas
that God was interested in showing favoritism among the nations or that God was committed to seeing that the "chosen"
people would be guaranteed health, wealth, and happiness, not
to mention power over everyone else in the world.

What Do You Understand About the Loaves?

The first word about understanding the loaves has already
been written. It is the word implicit in the story "A Day at the
Lake." The word was spoken by Jesus when He said, "Whoever
does not receive the kingdom of God as a child will not enter it"
(Mark 10:15). In spite of the conflict swirling around Jesus, finally intensifying into a tornado of murderous rage, there was
in the eye of the storm always a serene, joyous, refreshingly
simple yet powerful presence. Those who responded openly and
honestly to Jesus discovered within themselves a source of nur-
ture and satisfaction that hard work could never earn and religious living could never guarantee.

The feeding of the thousands had to do only incidentally with
loaves and fishes. This is what the disciples could not see. Jesus
saw clearly because He knew the Hebrew Scriptures well
enough to read beyond the historical account to its spiritual
meaning. Moses presided over a daily gift of "loaves" (manna)
in the desert. Yet when the story was recorded in Deuteronomy
8:1-3, the deeper meaning of the "loaves" was spelled out:

> Remember the long way that the Lord your God has led you
> these forty years in the wilderness, in order to humble you, test-
> ing you to know what was in your heart, whether or not you
> would keep his commandments. He humbled you by letting you
> hunger, then by feeding you with manna, . . . in order to make
> you understand that one does not live by bread alone, but by
> every word that comes from the mouth of the Lord.

A materialistic reading of the Israelites being fed with manna in the desert for forty years inspired the messianic hope that the Christ would produce economic miracles. A materialistic view of Jesus feeding the thousands in Galilee prompted the people to try to make Jesus their king on a platform of economic prosperity.

Jesus set them straight in a hurry:

> Very truly, I tell you, you are looking for me, not because you saw signs, but because you ate your fill of the loaves. Do not work for the food that perishes, but for the food that endures for eternal life, which the Son of Man will give you. For it is on him that God the Father has set his seal (John 6:26-27).

The people then tried to coerce Jesus into playing the magic game, reminding Him that their "fathers ate the manna in the wilderness." Jesus refused to be manipulated. Rejecting an exclusively literal interpretation of Scripture, He said, "It was not Moses who gave you the bread from heaven; but it is my Father who gives you the true bread from heaven. For the bread of God is that which comes down from heaven and gives life to the world" (John 6:32-33). When they asked Jesus for "this bread," He said: "I am the bread of life. Whoever comes to me will never be hungry, and whoever believes in me will never be thirsty" (John 6:35).

Wonderful! Now, everyone—the disciples first and also the religious leaders and the people—will understand about the loaves! Right? Oh, no. As soon as Jesus moved beyond an exclusively literal reading of the text to open its spiritual meaning, most of His hearers choked on "the bread" He was offering. We read next, "Because of this many of his disciples turned back and no longer went about with him" (John 6:66). "They did not understand about the loaves, but their hearts were hardened" (Mark 6:52).

What, then, does it take to "understand about the loaves?" Mark's account gives us the clue in adding the phrase, "but their hearts were hardened." The problem has to do with our hearts. The issue is not economics or politics. The issue is not obeying the law or traditions of worship. The issue is how to soften hardened hearts. The how is a choice: to open or to close our hearts to Jesus, whose presence is the presence of the living God. "Give us this bread" that "gives life to the world," the people asked. And Jesus said: "I am the bread of life!" (John 6:33-35). We understand about the loaves when we understand that, in the loaves, Jesus is giving us God's Spirit, God's Self!

Michael understood that he had been given a moment in the presence of God. His heart opened to God! He was fed in his spirit by the Spirit. He would never be the same again. Worry and fear would not have the same power over him. The adults did not understand because their hearts were closed to the presence who blessed the loaves and fed them. They saw the body of Jesus but were blind to His Spirit. Their hearts were closed to life. They ate of the loaves but were not fed by the Bread of life. What they had hardened was their childlike hearts—hearts that respond to the spirit of a person rather than to the person's public position or to the beliefs of society.

Here, then, is a great mystery. Why do people harden their hearts? Why do we lose touch with the inner child of our past? The thickening with which we harden our hearts is called scar tissue in medical usage. "Scar tissue" befits the wounds of the soul as well. A scar is the memory in the flesh of a wound. The hardening of a heart is the memory in the soul of a betrayal of trust—a betrayal that often has been buried in our past.

A boy grows up with an emotionally absent father. As a man he enters psychotherapy crippled because he has hardened his heart against intimacy within his family of marriage and with other men as well. He may enter spiritual direction with a minister complaining of the absence of God in spite of heroic efforts to be religious. His heart has become hard with hopelessness.

A girl is treated by her father like a second-class member of her family of origin. She may continue for decades to wait on the men in her world, to be submissive and to serve them. But she may never open her heart freely and fully to any man. She, too, may seek spiritual direction complaining of the failure of her faith to lift her out of her heavyheartedness. Her heart has hardened with the weight of servitude.

Popular media gives a lot of attention to possessive, domineering mothers. A more basic problem for the hard-hearted person may be absent or abusive fathers. No mother can possess or dominate a son or daughter unless the father's place in the family has become vacant. It may be equally true that no father can abuse son or daughter unless the mother's place has become similarly vacant. In any case, hardness of heart is a chronic condition with a long history that usually lies buried in the repressed memories of a person's childhood.

Is there any hope for the hard of heart? One sign on the way to hope is the ancient story of Pandora's box. When opened in response to curiosity, the contents of the box flew into the world like a covey of quail blasting out of their brushy cover. Evermore the world has been filled with anger and hate, with grief and despair, with gluttony and greed, with lust and cruelty, with conspiracy, deception, and betrayal. In the end, Pandora took one last look into the box. There remained hope.

This is the story of the adventure into spiritual maturity. It is true for individuals and for groups, organizations, nations, and world religions alike. First our destructive passions run their course, corrupting every utopian scheme ever devised. Then, at last, we find hope. With modest goals, realism about our limits, and confidence in the cosmic Architect of human history, we discover another passion: our desire for God.

Then we know that the conflict between hard and mellow hearts is a conflict of desires. Every desire that constricts, binds our minds, chokes our compassion, consumes and wastes our energies, and, in short, shrivels our souls as scar tissue is generated to enclose and protect a hardening heart. Desires that open us, generate good will, honor honest differences, invite communion, trust, and openness to mutual growth and change are desires nourishing a vibrant and healthy heart.

We can spot the desires of a hardened heart by certain telltale signs: (1) They need to be indulged more and more in order to give satisfaction. (2) These desires punish us with withdrawal symptoms if they are not fed. (3) Worst of all, they inspire mind games of self-deception and dishonesty with others designed to justify our indulgences. We may recognize in these signs the familiar addictions to alcohol and drug abuse. Most of us hide our wounded—and hardening—hearts under less obvious desires. We may be chronically angry or avid collectors of art. We may be driven by desires for candy or for noble causes and by ambition or the meaning of dreams. We may have insatiable desires for food or friends, memories or money, pets or popcorn. Conflicts with others may prompt us to desire above all positive relationships or cruel revenge. Enslaving and heart-hardening desires may include shoplifting or sleeping, television or tobacco, weight loss or work, sex or spiritual disciplines. Let any of these desires become central in our lives, and we are on the way to becoming hard-hearted, blind to the presence of God, and closed to God's heart-nourishing gifts.

In contrast, consider the desire for the God of perfect love. Fulfillment energizes us with compassion and creativity, spontaneity and joy. It empowers us with courage for taking risks. A strong attachment to the God of love links us with other people, with all God's creatures, and with the created universe—not as a means to our own ends but as ends in themselves. Withdrawal of our desires for God allows the desire to cool without the typical withdrawal symptoms. We are free to turn away if we wish.

In a word, the desire for God breaks down the walls that separate us from others, unlocks the prison of a hardened heart, and frees us to get on with the Christian adventure, which may be called a pilgrimage toward home. Home, in this sense, is where our inmost selves, our desires and our wills, live together in harmony with the Creator and with the whole creation.

The desire for God is not an escape from the conflicts, wounds, and failures of life in the real world. On the contrary, it is an option that is altogether practical and available in coping with the crises as well as the mundane and the humdrum in everyday living.

Dangers beset us in giving ourselves to our desires for God. Our desires for God may inflate our sense of self-importance or feed the heart-hardening feeling of self-righteousness. The experience of the presence of God is a powerful antidote, however, especially when we stay close to the Jesus story as told in the Gospels. Our newly awakened desire for God creates the possibility of shifting our center from self-importance to a wholehearted surrender to the Spirit of God within. We discover in our own experiences the paradox of finding ourselves by losing ourselves in the God of love.

Serious seekers after God quickly discover that their desires for God may sharpen the pain before relieving it. The complaint I hear most often from those who are drawn to me for spiritual direction is: "Why is God so absent, even though I am seeking God desperately?" For these, the desire for God heightens their distress, sharpens the pain of old wounds, and stimulates confusion about making sense of life in the everyday world.

For some, the very word *God* calls to mind the faces of people who have abused, abandoned, or otherwise crippled them. They are in the grip of primitive god images. While they can think about a God of both power and love, they do not experience God as such. The god of their experience is a tyrant, a deceiver, a rapist, or a wimp. Once such persons have become part of a group who care for one another without cruelty and manipulation, they can begin to see that the god they have known in the past is a mask on the face of evil. Then at last, desire for the true God can begin to stir.

An active desire for God gets some people into big trouble because of the groups to which they attach themselves in their search. For one it may be a group experimenting with street drugs in the name of spirituality. For another, the group may be highly disciplined and genuinely seeking God, but they may require all who enter to check in their minds at the door. Blind obedience can relieve people from the pain of seeking meaning in life, but it also can block them from ever knowing what it is to love God "with all your mind." In the end the devotees of such religious groups become more and more discouraged and lose contact with their inmost selves. They lose, thereby, their most precious treasure. They lose the power "to love the Lord your God with all your heart, and with all your soul, and and with all your mind, and with all your strength" (Mark 12:30).

In the light of this discussion of the conflict between desires, we return to the starting point of "understanding about the loaves." Jesus tried to open His critics to understand the loaves by showing them the error of a shallow reading of Scripture that shuts itself off from the piercing spiritual truths contained in the Word. Rather than opening their hearts to Jesus, they closed them even tighter, hardening their hearts.

Clearly, this superficial use of God's Word is another symptom of the hardened heart. Applied to the Christian adventure, it is a deadly prescription. It often misses the deeper meaning of Scripture and allows us to escape applying its truth to our own lives. It fosters the desire to continue to hide one's wounds by any means, to avoid communication with one's inmost self. What frightens a person is that the old wounds lie buried close to one's spiritual center. Like an image in Bunyan's *Pilgrim's Progress*, the approach to the House Beautiful is guarded by two lions. From a distance they frighten one away. On drawing close, one sees that they are chained in place and cannot harm the pilgrim who stays on the path up to the door of the house.

Perhaps God's love faces no more difficult challenge than to touch and transform us who protect our hurt and hardened hearts with a shallow, "disarmed," use of Scripture. For when we sift the Scripture, retaining only the words and casting aside the deeper spiritual meanings, God's love cannot affect us. In fact, this use of Scripture actually drives us further away from God, making us even more calloused and hard. Jesus described the problem well. When the Pharisees of His day asked, "Surely we are not blind, are we?" Jesus replied, "If you were blind, you would not have sin. But now that you say, 'We see,' your sin remains" (John 9:41).

With God, however, all things are possible. Saul of Tarsus was captive to the desire for power and praise among the religious leaders of his day. He was the inquisitor in the first generation after the death and resurrection of Jesus. His heart was hardened, indeed, against the Jesus who appeared to him on the Damascus Road. Yet Saul surrendered himself to Jesus wholeheartedly, transformed the early church from a Jewish sect to a universal faith, and continued the conflict with those whose hearts were both wounded and hardened. Pleading with the church of Corinth to understand, Paul gave witness: "Our competence is from God, who has made us competent to be ministers of a new covenant, not of letter but of spirit; for the letter kills, but the Spirit gives life" (2 Cor. 3:5-6).

The discovery of a ten-year-old boy, Michael, during "A Day at the Lake" has proven to be a word of hope in the midst of a misunderstanding about Scripture that generated murderous rage against Jesus and also against Paul in the earliest days of the Christian adventure. The conflict flares up anew in the life of all such adventurers of every age. At the heart of the conflict is a choice of desires. In the presence of God, everything depends on "understanding about the loaves." It all has to do with our desires—a desire to protect our wounded and hardened hearts or a desire to be melted down by the presence until every desire finds its place within desire for the gift of God's Self as the Bread of life.

Notes

1. Passages of Scripture in a "A Day at the Lake" are quoted or modified from: *The Cotton Patch Version of Matthew and John*, and *The Cotton Patch Version of Luke and Acts*, trans. Clarence Jordan (New York: Association Press, 1970, 1969).

5

Set for Suffering

In the next act of the Jesus drama, death comes center stage. We leave behind the meadows of Galilee, the wonder of healing, the calming of storms at sea and within the hearts of the people, the hospitality of feeding the thousands. We enter a wild and rugged, dark and stormy time. Jesus shifted His focus from conflict with the rigidity of legalistic rules that were starving the souls of the people to a dread that had hardened the hearts of His disciples. His target became the universal dread of death.

Opposition at this point flared up not from the legal scholars and the defenders of the Torah, but from His own disciples. The questions Jesus pressed with them were essentially the same that we saw following the feeding of the five thousand: Who am I? What am I about? What sort of kingdom am I announcing? But a new word enters the picture: what sort of kingdom is worth *dying* for? As Jesus began to challenge His disciples to see the link between a kingdom of love and the reality of death—for Himself and for them—conflict erupted like a volcano.

Before entering the story of this conflict as it flared up between Jesus and Peter, let us step back and take a look at a hero story of an even more ancient time in which the central conflict was between the hero, Gilgamesh, and death. The similarities and differences between Gilgamesh and Jesus are most instructive for everyone on a journey driven by desire for God.

The Epic of Gilgamesh[1]

The oldest recorded story of a spiritual journey is the Babylo-
·nian epic of Gilgamesh. The legend was as old at the time of
Homer as Homer's *Iliad* and *Odyssey* are to us today. As the
story opens, we see Gilgamesh, who is part man and part god,
ruling as king of Uruk. He meets a savage named Enkidu who is
part man and part animal. They wrestle, and Gilgamesh wins;
but immediately they become "like brothers." As a team they
are invincible. So they set out to kill the evil monster, Hum-
baba. They intend to destroy evil and so to immortalize
themselves.

The gods are threatened, however, and decree that Enkidu
must die. Gilgamesh does not know what death is until his
friend dies. He becomes bitter and afraid, but resolves never to
experience death himself. Instead he sets out on a journey to
find the gods and wrest from them the secret of immortality.

As symbols of the human condition, the story shows the
power of people who combine both their animal and their divine potentials. It shows the power of evil in the hostility of the
gods who intervene to prevent human beings from maintaining
harmonious integration of both their animal and their godly na-
tures. The story uncovers the passion of everyone for immortality. Anxiety about aging and death arises out of the shadows of
denial and repression to become the driving force of the Gilgamesh story. Who does not identify with the hero as he sets out
on this desperate journey, hoping against hope that he will
overcome aging and death and bring back to his people both
immortality and a new depth of meaning in life?

Gilgamesh, like Jesus, is a heroic figure. He is a legendary
man-god. So the stage is set for conflict between a man-god and
death. The plot unfolds in a series of trials on the journey. First
Gilgamesh gets through a gate into mountains that are wrapped
in utter darkness. Traveling in darkness presents Gilgamesh
with his first trial. So it is with everyone who seeks direct encounter with God. The way is dark and lonely. The traveler is

forced to rely on guidance from within one's self. Expressways with their lighted green road signs do not cut through these mountains.

Gilgamesh perseveres and eventually comes into a garden of the gods, bathed in sunshine and presided over by Siduri, "the woman of the vine, the maker of wine." Siduri presents him with a different test. "What's your hurry?" she asks. "You will never find that life for which you are looking. When the gods created man they allotted to him death, but life they retained in their own keeping." "So," she urges, "fill your belly with good things; day and night, night and day, dance and be merry, feast and rejoice. Let your clothes be fresh, bathe yourself in water, cherish the little child that holds your hand, and make your wife happy in your embrace; for this too is the lot of man."

Gilgamesh is not swayed. Instead he extracts from her the name of the ferryman who alone crosses the ocean of death to the realm of Utnapishtim, who holds the secret of immortality. The third trial is crossing the ocean without being touched by the waters of death.

Early successes in getting through times of struggle and the darkness of discouragement often inspire feelings of having earned the right to indulge oneself. Many a seeker after God gives up on the quest by mid-life, settling for the pleasures and security of family and friends, good food, work, and leisure. Some, however, press on, venturing out onto the depths of life in spite of the danger of being swallowed up—"being touched by the waters of death."

The third trial suggests to a modern-day reader a journey of depth psychotherapy or the development of ancient disciplines of "praying without ceasing," of entering a state of God-consciousness in which a person is briefly at one with all that is. In such experiences, the traveler must risk losing ego control and being carried by deep psychic and cosmic forces across a trackless sea to a distant shore where the future cannot be known for certain. The dangers of "being touched by the waters of death" might well fit the "ego death" experience out of which comes profound inner transformation.

In any event, Gilgamesh reaches the far shore safely and finds Utnapishtim who has the power to reveal to him the "secret of the gods" whereby Utnapishtim himself achieved immortality. The secret is that Utnapishtim won immortality as a gift of the gods for his obedience in saving a remnant in his ark at the time of the flood. What he offers Gilgamesh is one more trial: to prevail against sleep for six days and seven nights.

That the ultimate test is to stay awake almost indefinitely is no surprise to the person on a spiritual journey. The image of being awake is widely used to describe a high level of God-consciousness. Whereas anyone can experience the real presence of God in fleeting moments of awakeness, who can remain in such a state of awareness indefinitely? Gilgamesh undertakes the ultimate test confident that he can succeed where all others have failed. In no time, however, he falls asleep and sleeps for seven days.

As a consolation prize, he is transformed from an old man into a person in the prime of life and told how to find a flower that will keep him in perpetual youth. Gilgamesh finds the flower and begins the return journey home.

We come now to the turning point of the plot. Gilgamesh has not achieved immortality, but he has gained the secret of perpetual youth. He has proved himself to be a person of steadfast purpose, remarkable self-discipline, and matchless courage; but he has failed the ultimate test of one's desire for God. Courage and self-control he has in heroic measure, but the ability to maintain a steady state of God-consciousness he lacks.

At this point we connect with the theme of the desire for God. Gilgamesh has made his choice and set his priorities in life. His goal is to "save his life" and if possible to bring back from the gods the secret of immortality for his people as well. His desire for God is self-centered. In the terms of Bernard of Clairvaux, Gilgamesh is at the stage of loving God for self's sake. He knows nothing of loving God for God's sake, nor of loving self for God's sake, which is an even higher stage of spiritual maturity.

As to his method or "plan of salvation," Gilgamesh relies entirely on his own powers. He mobilizes his godlike abilities for the journey and relies on his cleverness to persuade Utnapishtim to reveal the secret of the gods. Utnapishtim tells him that immortality is a gift to be received, not a prize to be won, but Gilgamesh cannot accept this word. He commits himself to take the ultimate test and, as we have seen, fails completely. No wonder he cannot maintain his state of being spiritually awake. He has never really understood his place in relation to God. He knows nothing of the willingness to be loved and transformed by God for God's own pleasure. His desire for God is deficient, his awareness of God undeveloped. Surrender to God in radical dependence on the lordship and gifts of God is impossible, for Gilgamesh believes that he is God's equal.

As we return to the story, we find that Gilgamesh pauses on his journey home to bathe in a deep pool. A serpent, sensing the sweetness of the flower of perpetual youth that Gilgamesh carries, rises out of the water, snatches the flower, immediately sloughs off its skin, and returns to the bottom of the pool.

Gilgamesh sits down and weeps; then rises up and returns home to live as a king, but finally to die and be buried like all others before him—and since.

The resolution of the conflict in the Gilgamesh epic is a whimper rather than a victory celebration. The heroism of Gilgamesh becomes finally his resignation to aging and death rather than their conquest.

We shall return to the Gilgamesh epic after turning next to the Jesus story. In reading the story, "The Second Sight," let yourself imagine that a recent archaeological dig uncovered a diary that was kept by Simon Peter during the days of Jesus' earthly ministry. The following pages from that diary offer us a look into a few days, at the peak of Jesus' ministry, when He began to challenge His disciples to face the reality of His impending death and to view death for themselves and all people in a radically different way.

After some comments on the story, we conclude the chapter with some comparisons and contrasts between the two accounts as they inform those of us today whose journey through life is a Christian adventure.

Story: The Second Sight

Tuesday—In Bethsaida

Back again to these bleak highlands out of Bethsaida. I don't know why Jesus insists on coming here. The crowds always find us.

[Editor's Note: These highlands are about two miles northeast of Bethsaida on the east bank of the Sea of Galilee, also called the Lake of Gennesaret.]

Some retreat! Over five thousand famished folk blew us out of our "retreat" a few weeks ago, and yesterday a repeat performance. Of course, things are getting better. Only four thousand barged in on our supposed "retreat" this time.

Jesus is sure getting hard to live with these days. Ever since He found us mystified about what He did with that kids' lunch—feeding that crowd with five loaves and two fish!—He has been a bear. It wasn't so bad when He was reaming out the Pharisees, but lately He's been dumping on us:

"Do you not yet perceive or understand?"

"Are your hearts hardened?"

"Having eyes do you not see, and having ears do you not hear?"

What's He getting at? Why can't the man just come out and say what He wants us to make of all this theology business? Why all this, "Do you not yet understand" business? Why is He getting so irritable with us?

I'm confused. I'm sick and tired of feeling stupid all the time. Like today. We finally got back to civilization [in Bethsaida], and this "official delegation" brought the blind brother of the ruler of the synagogue for Jesus to give him back his sight. So what does Jesus do but lead the blind man by the hand out of town. He won't let the "officialdom" follow us out there. Jesus does His laying on of hands, and the poor guy says, "I can see men, but they look like trees walking." So He does it a second time, and the man can see clearly; but then He won't let the man go into the village even, but sends him home another way.

Now, what's going on? I don't get it. Yesterday Jesus feeds another crowd of thousands with seven loaves, and today he bungles His first try at giving a man sight. Is that why He didn't let the delegation come with us? Was He unsure of this one? Or is He just trying to keep down the mass hysteria that is swamping us and turning us all into a bunch of bickering kids. It scares me because the Teacher is changing, and I don't understand why.

So, we shall see what tomorrow will bring . . .

Thursday—En Route to Caesarea Philippi

At last, Jesus gave up on the east coast of Galilee, and we headed north toward Caesarea Philippi. What a place! Romantic is the only word for it. Such natural beauty, it takes your breath away—and revives your spirits too. How we needed this. Finally, a real retreat in the offing.

Friday—On retreat

Jesus can take His messiahship and stuff it! I've had it with Him and this whole movement. The Man is going to destroy everything we have built since we joined His team. "Son of Man" He calls Himself. Does He think we are a bunch of illiterates? We know the prophecies too. The Book of Daniel says it plain: The Son of Man shall have dominion over all peoples, nations, and languages, and the kingdom shall not be destroyed.

[Editor's Note: The reference to which Peter refers is Daniel 7:13-14.]

Has He deliberately deceived us, calling Himself the Son of Man? Or is He self-deceived? Maybe it doesn't matter which it is. The bottom line is that this whole movement is going to self-destruct if He keeps on talking about being killed. What hurts me most is . . . is the way He turned on me. I came up to Him privately, just man to man. I tried to talk some political sense into His head—to help Him see what He was doing to the whole movement with that kind of defeatist thinking. He sees the other fellows coming in close, listening in, and He turns on me. Booms out so everyone can hear: "Get behind me, Satan!" *Satan?* He called me Satan. Me, Simon Peter, the "Rock"! Just this morning He nicknamed me "The Rock." And before the day ends, I am Satan?

What does the Man have against me? Never, never has He spoken that way to any one of us in the movement. And in front of everyone—making a fool as well as a villain of me. Can He be so blind? Doesn't He realize what I have done for His movement? Who does He think it is that holds this group of young turks together? Without me on top of things, they would split apart into rival factions in no time. I could tell Him right now, if He were listening instead of calling people names, that those Zebedee brothers [James and John] are blind with ambition. If He isn't careful, they will rip this thing wide open in no time.

This morning it came to me in a flash. Jesus was pumping us: "Who do they say that I am?" He kept asking us. And I saw it—all at once I saw it. Jesus is the Messiah! In that split second, everything made sense: the healings, walking on water, calming the winds, and even the loaves—especially the loaves! Moses did it. Elijah did it. Jesus fulfills both the Law and the Prophets!

"And I tell you," He said, "you are Peter, and on this rock I will build my church, and the powers of death shall not prevail against it." And then about the keys: "Whatever you bind on earth shall be bound in heaven," and "whatever you loose on earth shall be loosed in heaven." Would He give the keys—

whatever that means—to Satan? It's too crazy. It makes no sense. Maybe I just need to get out while the gettin's good.

Friday [*One Week Later*]

One week ago today my words came hot and heavy. Today I can hardly find words to write. One week ago my feelings were hurt. I was ready to quit. Today, I am His forever! Last week, Jesus made a fool of me. Today, I made a fool of myself. But it doesn't matter, it doesn't matter at all.

He took only James and John [the Zebedee brothers] and me to the mountain. He never said a word all morning as we climbed. Finally, we sat down, aching and ready to eat our lunches, when it happened. How can I possibly find the words to record it?

It was as if the noonday sun were suddenly inside Jesus' body—a radiance from within, more than a lamp on Him from outside. In one way He looked the same, but what we saw was His soul, His spirit. Only it was so much more. His spirit was God's Spirit. The light was blinding and burning but not hot or harsh. His face shown, like Moses coming down the mountain with the Commandments. And His garments too. They were whiter than white, radiant, resplendent—beyond words.

Moses and Elijah were there too. The three of them were talking. The Zebedee boys said I blurted out: "Master, let's make 'three booths, one for you and one for Moses and one for Elijah.' " Big mouth, me. I don't remember anything but my terror and awe. I do remember that a dark cloud settled suddenly on the mountain, and then a voice came: "This is my beloved Son; listen to him." Then, as quickly as it came, the cloud lifted, and no one was there except Jesus and the three of us.

I don't know which is the greater marvel: what we saw or the way I now feel about Jesus, and also about James and John. Jesus? I called Him Master when I didn't know what I was saying up on the mountain, but I will call Him Master from now on—and mean it! James and John? I like the characters now! We feel closer than brothers. The movement is in no danger of falling apart now, I'm certain.

Coming down, Jesus didn't stop talking. And did He ever open our eyes. He recited the Servant poems from Isaiah—from memory. He showed us that the Son of man prophecies in Daniel have to be understood in relation to the Suffering Servant in Isaiah. [Editor's Note: The reference is to Isaiah 53.] Then He kept talking about rising from the dead and the need for us all to be crucified as we follow Him.

James tells me that this talk is all metaphor. The cross is a Roman form of torture that we Jews would never use against our worst enemies. So the cross stands for having our inner, spiritual oppression destroyed in our loyalty to Jesus. The Messiah is going to overthrow Roman rule and set up a spiritual kingdom—somehow. If James is right, then all this talk about dying and rising again, being rejected and despised, is just getting us ready for the freedom fight we are heading into together.

On the other hand, John says there are dark days ahead for Jesus and for all of us. John says Jesus would not have exploded at me the day He called me Satan if He were talking in metaphors about a freedom fight against Rome. Well, I cannot get used to the idea that God could want anything other than for Jesus to be successful in bringing in the kingdom of God. After all, He is making it clear that the kingdom of God is a new way of life for everybody. It's not just political, I know that now. But how can it not be political as well as spiritual if the spiritual part is to work?

Come to think of it, I'm like that blind man back in Bethsaida after Jesus touched Him the first time. I can see who Jesus is, the promised Messiah, but the rest of the story is like trees walking. Maybe I could do with some second sight too.

Comments on Story: The Second Sight

The Action

External action in "The Second Sight" must be inferred from entries in the diary, but the action within Peter holds the spotlight. In a word, Peter suffers an ego wound. Hurt and humiliated, Peter wants to quit. He was ready to get out of the Jesus movement "while the gettin's good."

This complication in the unfolding of the story builds gradually. It begins in mild frustration at the pressure the crowds are putting on the leadership of the movement. Just as the disciples return from their first mission of preaching, teaching, and healing, flushed with success, they learn of the murder of John the Baptist—in cold blood. The glow of their success turns suddenly to ashes. Jesus knows they need to get away. They, too, are vulnerable to the lawless hand of Herod the Great. They must grieve John's death and regroup for the next phase of their mission. They desperately need time away, time alone with each other and with Jesus. Twice they go on retreat, and twice crowds of thousands follow and swallow them up in their neediness.

To make matters worse, Jesus gets upset with them. Mark tells us what brought on Jesus' frustration. Jesus had fed more than five thousand people with five loaves and two fish. Soon after, He again fed thousands, this time with seven loaves and "a few small fish." Almost immediately, they took a boat again for the other side of the Sea of Galilee. The disciples "had forgotten to bring any bread; and they had only one loaf with them in the boat" (8:14). Jesus used a food analogy in warning them to "beware of the leaven of the Pharisees and the leaven of Herod"; but the disciples missed the whole point and started discussing with each other, saying, "We have no bread." Jesus jumped them. Mark quotes Him, saying,

Why are you talking about having no bread? Do you still not perceive or understand? Are your hearts hardened? Do you have eyes, and fail to see? Do you have ears, and fail to hear? And do you not remember? When I broke the five loaves for the five thousand, how many baskets full of broken pieces did you collect? . . . And the seven for the four thousand, how many baskets full of broken pieces did you collect? . . . Do you not yet understand? (Mark 8:14-21)

So, what does Peter do with this rebuke? He projects the blindness and the failure of faith on the part of the disciples right back onto Jesus. He writes in his diary about the very next event, the giving of sight to a blind man in Bethsaida, blaming Jesus for a failure of faith. Peter wrote, "I don't get it . . . He bungles His first try at giving a man sight . . . Was He so unsure of Himself on this one?"

By the time they reach Caesarea Philippi, Peter has swallowed his anger. No doubt the natural beauty of the place and freedom from the crowds have relaxed him. In the seminar the next morning, Peter shines. Jesus is asking who people say that He is. Peter sees into the mystery of Jesus' messiahship first: Jesus is not a reincarnation of John the Baptist or of Elijah but in fact, the promised Messiah. Peter is feeling smug, imagining that he is head of the class!

Then, in the middle of the afternoon seminar, tempers flare. Jesus has begun the course on "advanced messiahship," as it were. He is bearing down on the theme "that the Son of Man must undergo great suffering, and be rejected by the elders, the chief priests, and the scribes, and be killed, and after three days rise again." Mark added, "He said all this quite openly." Peter understood it clearly, "And Peter took him aside and began to rebuke him." The word that Mark uses, "rebuke," implies physical assault, such as a rabbi rapping the knuckles of a student, or one person shaking another by the shoulders in a temper. Then one rebuke led to another, for Jesus "rebuked Peter," saying, "Get behind me, Satan! For you are setting your mind not on divine things but on human things" (Mark 8:31-33). Perhaps Jesus took hold of Peter's shoulders and shook him or even threw Peter behind Him with a wrestler's move. Whatever actually happened, it was a tense moment for the entire group that day—a moment Peter at least never forgot (Mark 8:31-32).

How did Jesus respond? Nothing in Mark's account suggests that Jesus tried to put salve on Peter's wounded ego. Instead, Jesus used the tension of the moment to make a dramatic turn in His preaching ministry. He sounded a new theme: "If any want to become my followers, let them deny themselves and take up their cross and follow me. For those who want to save their life will lose it, and those who lose their life for my sake, and the sake of the gospel, will save it" (Mark 8:34-35).

In the heat of the tempest, Peter concludes in his diary, "Maybe I just need to get out while the gettin's good." He, and perhaps other disciples as well have come to a parting of the ways. Morale could not be worse. The solidarity of the movement is in doubt.

Six days later, the resolution comes. Jesus takes with Him Peter, James, and John up a high mountain alone. Are these the leaders of rival factions forming within the movement? Is this Jesus' strategic response to the ruckus in the afternoon seminar? We cannot say, but what Mark makes clear is that, when they come down from the mountain, they are no longer challenging Jesus' vision of His messiahship. Subsequent events make it clear they still did not accept the reality of His being killed and rising from the dead, but the leaders of the movement are together. "The movement is in no danger of falling apart now," concludes Peter, "I'm certain."

The Characters

"The Second Sight" is a story about two primary characters: Peter and Jesus. At one level they are remarkably alike. Both are passionate, intense, and capable of aggressively defending fundamental issues in the mission they shared. Peter is impatient with Jesus' challenge to the popular hope of a political campaign. Jesus is weary with the blindness of His disciples, their resistance to seeing the clear meaning of His deeds as signs of His own identity and the clues to the nature of the kingdom He was establishing on earth. Both Peter and Jesus are passionately loyal to their own vision of things.

Where are they different? Peter is centered on the defense of his own ego—his place among the disciples, his stardom as a leader, and his need to look good in his own eyes. To defend himself, Peter projects his own faults on to Jesus, blames others before looking at his own failures. When he gets upset, he throws his weight around. He even tries to intimidate Jesus rather than to think about the matters in dispute between them.

Jesus' focus is not on His own ego but on the problem of preparing His disciples for the ordeal that is just ahead for them all. He is clear and straight with them about His vision, and when push comes to shove, He is tough and uncompromising. He gives His closest disciples permission to leave if they must, but He requires that they be willing to take up a cross—be prepared to die as common criminals—if they stay true. What we see of the inner character of Peter and Jesus at this point in the story proves to be true for both of them in the final showdown that is soon to come in Jerusalem.

Central Themes

Four themes call for special attention in "The Second Sight." The first is the question Jesus asked His disciples: "Who do men say that I am?" This includes the questions of messiahship and of Jesus' identity. Jesus was referring to Himself consistently as "the Son of man." A primary source in the Hebrew Scriptures is a passage in Daniel 7:13-14:

> I saw one like a human being
> coming with the clouds of heaven.
> And he came to the Ancient One
> and was presented before him.
> To him was given dominion
> and glory and kingship,
> that all peoples, nations, and languages

should serve him.
His dominion is an everlasting dominion,
that shall not pass away,
and his kingship is one
that shall never be destroyed.

This passage and others like it were well known to the people of
the time. For most, the "Son of man" image shaped a view of
the future in which a messiah would not only deliver Israel from
oppression but also rule the world, with Israel as His chosen
people.

Over against the "Son of man" are the Isaiah passages about
the "Suffering Servant." It is this image that informed Jesus'
view of His own mission as He began to teach them at Caesarea
Philippi. Representative of the Suffering Servant poems are
these words from Isaiah 53:3-5:

He was despised and rejected by others;
a man of suffering and acquainted with infirmity;
and as one from whom others hide their faces
he was despised, and we held him of no account.

Surely he has borne our infirmities
and carried our diseases;
yet we accounted him stricken,
struck down by God, and afflicted.
But he was wounded for our transgressions,
crushed for our iniquities;
upon him was the punishment that made us whole,
and by his bruises we are healed.

So the most obvious theme of the story is the conflict between
these two visions of who Jesus is and what He is about.

Next, is the theme of the need for second sight. As Mark reported it, Peter saw with partial sight—as if seeing "people . . .
like trees, walking" (8:24). Peter saw that Jesus was Messiah,
Son of man, but not that Jesus was Messiah, Suffering Servant.
Confessing Jesus to be Messiah, Peter saw only the militant,

imperial messiah of the Daniel passage. Peter's outburst or "rebuke" of Jesus was prompted by Jesus' new teaching that "the Son of Man must undergo great suffering, and be rejected by the elders, the chief priests, and the scribes, and be killed, and after three days rise again" (8:31). After the mystic experience on the mount of transfiguration, Peter began to come to terms with the idea of a Messiah who might suffer and be killed by His enemies. Even then, however, Peter showed no evidence (in Mark's Gospel) of being able wholeheartedly to confess: "You are the Son of God."

Actually, then, in the biblical account, we find three levels of *insight* into the mystery of Jesus, the Christ (Messiah). The first level is seeing Jesus as the divinely appointed political deliverer of Israel. This is literal seeing, bound by the see-touch world. The second level is seeing Jesus as God's Suffering Servant, establishing a kingdom of the spirit in which God works to transform people into godlikeness in love. A third level of seeing fathoms the mystery of Jesus as the Son of God. At this level, a person experiences Jesus, the Christ, as the presence of God in the world, "bruised for our iniquities" and by whose "stripes we are healed" (Isa. 53:5, KJV). At this level of *insight,* God is known to be in Jesus, offering understanding and acceptance to all, even to the little people of the world, those oppressed by religion and by government, even to forgiving, accepting, and loving criminals, among whom God in Christ was crucified.

Equally obvious in the story is a third theme: that desire for God grows in spurts of awareness, from crisis to crisis, according as a person is able to see. We, like the blind man of Bethsaida, must be prepared to "see people . . . like trees, walking" at first. We need to develop patience and the courageous willingness to let God shatter some of our favorite beliefs before our sight can be fully healed. We have only begun the Christian adventure when we see into the mystery of Jesus as the Christ, the Son of the living God. Seeing into the darker mystery calls for "second sight." For eyes to see that we too must embrace death. We must take up the cross and lose our lives for the sake of Jesus and the gospel.

Here, then, is a fourth level of *insight* and the fourth major theme of the story as well. Applying the story to our lives today, we see at once that discipleship is costly. Desire for God does not thrive in the soil of a convenient and comfortable discipleship. Desire for God grows in taking up our own cross and following Jesus. What is involved is much more than one heroic decision to become a disciple. What is involved is a new lifestyle. Jesus' message to the people centered on a radical change of values. Immediately after His harsh encounter with Peter, Jesus called "the multitude" to Him and said:

> If any want to become my followers, let them deny themselves and take up their cross and follow me. For those who want to save their life will lose it, and those who lose their life for my sake, and the sake of the gospel, will save it. For what will it profit to gain the whole world and forfeit their life? Indeed, what can they give in return for their life?" (Mark 8:34-37).

In our time, the call to costly discipleship comes most clearly out of the resistance movement against the Nazi tyranny in Germany in the mid-1940s. Dietrich Bonhoeffer, whose discipleship led to his death at the hands of the Nazis, wrote:

> Cheap grace is the deadly enemy of our Church. We are fighting today for costly grace. . . . Cheap grace is the preaching of forgiveness without requiring repentance, baptism without Church discipline, Communion without confession, absolution without contrition. Cheap grace is grace without discipleship, grace without the Cross, grace without Jesus Christ, living and incarnate.[2]

In Paul's letter to the church at Corinth we see costly grace celebrated as a new life-style built on the model of "Christ crucified."

Where is the one who is wise? Where is the scribe? Where is the debater of this age? Has not God made foolish the wisdom of the world? For since, in the wisdom of God, the world did not know God through wisdom, God decided, through the foolishness of our proclamation, to save those who believe. For Jews demand signs and Greeks desire wisdom, but we proclaim Christ crucified, a stumbling block to Jews and foolishness to Gentiles, but to those who are the called, both Jews and Greeks, Christ the power of God and the wisdom of God. For God's foolishness is wiser than human wisdom, and God's weakness is stronger than human strength (1 Cor. 1:20-25).

The mystery of faith is not veiled at this point. Within the Jesus story, the kind of "seeing" that matters most is not "the wisdom of the world." The *insight* of prime importance is seeing beyond the trauma of Christ crucified on a Roman cross into the scandal of God being put to death as a common criminal at the will of a religious establishment and by the hand of the state. This kind of seeing is not the function of the optic nerves, but of the psychic and spiritual nerve to be a disciple.

Desire for God

At Caesarea Philippi, we come to the decisive parting of the ways in the Jesus story. Jesus takes the road less traveled, the way of the Suffering Servant. Begrudgingly and without understanding why, the disciples follow. The road they travel from here on has only one destination: crucifixion on a Roman cross. What happens on such a road to the desire for God? What could happen had Jesus chosen to go for fame and immortality? How does the Jesus story compare with the Gilgamesh epic as to the human struggle to overcome death?

Gilgamesh sees death as an enemy to be conquered. After his traumatic failure, he sees aging and death as involuntary suffering to be accepted insofar as possible. He remains a heroic figure even in failure, for he courageously accepts death as the lot of humankind. He models for his people the heroism of accepting life on its own terms.

Jesus sees death as a destiny to be chosen, a calling to be fulfilled. He accepts it to be sure, but His acceptance is voluntary.
This makes all the difference. His heroism is the courage to be
true to His vision of the presence of God as perfect love in an
imperfect world. The self-protective and evil side of life—
shaped by the institutions of religion and of government, in particular—cannot tolerate perfect love. A prophet of love, then,
must be prepared to die and leave the results to God. Desire for
immortality feeds a person's pride and so increases the realm of
evil. Desire for God renounces the arbitrary use of power over
others. It displaces one's wish to be immune from the disease of
mortality with delight in the presence of God within the here
and now.

For Jesus, death is not a subject for philosophical discussion.
It is a Roman cross on which to be humiliated and tortured. For
the followers of Christ, the literal meaning of the cross is primary, as well. Literally it means taking a stand with all of those
who are despised, feared, exploited, oppressed, and shut out of
polite society, who are denied respect and the privileges that
come with wealth and status. A disciple of Christ who was not a
Roman citizen could be put to death as a common criminal or
on a charge of high treason as an enemy of the empire. This was,
in fact, the fate of many of the early readers of the Gospels.
Converts from Judaism were excommunicated from their synagogues, and thereby they too became vulnerable to crucifixion.
Jews were exempt from crucifixion under Roman law, but
Christians were not. Even a Roman citizen who refused to worship the emperor as god was marked as an enemy of the state
and subject to a death sentence.

In time, Christianity became legal, but crucifixion has been
historically imprinted in the Christian psyche. Taking up one's
cross and following Jesus is the heart of life within the Jesus
story. The first step on that journey for us, as for Peter and the
other disciples at Caesarea Philippi, is to reflect on our level of
"sight" as to who Jesus was and who Jesus is today.

What, for instance, was your level of understanding on your

"first sight" of Jesus? What then changed when you received your "second sight"? At what level of "sight" are you now? Third sight? Fourth sight? How has your understanding of Jesus changed through the years? Parallel to the question about who Jesus is, you may ask yourself the second question: What is my level of "sight" about the kingdom Jesus has established on earth? What does it mean to pray, "Thy Kingdom come. Thy will be done in earth, as it is in heaven" (KJV)?

It may be that your level of seeing into the mystery of death is a measure of your spiritual growth. Dread of death as *the* enemy hardens your heart, blinds your eyes, and closes your ears against the presence of the Christ. Voluntary choice of death to self means to surrender ego control to the God of your "second sight." This surrender opens your heart, your eyes, and your ears to God's transforming presence in your inmost self, and in your institutional commitments as well.

Notes

1. *The Epic of Gilgamesh,* introduction by N. K. Sandars (New York: Penguin Books, 1960, 1972).

2. For Bonhoeffer's full discussion of this theme, see *The Cost of Discipleship* (New York: Macmillan, 1963).

6

A Fool for God

Every event in the life of Jesus poses a single question and forces the same choice. The question: Who is Jesus? The choice: Will you believe and become His disciple, or will you go your way in unbelief? These issues come to a climax in the crucifixion. The final challenge to Jesus is death, and the darkest mystery for disciples of Jesus is wrapped in suffering and death. Desire for God brings a person to the cross today, just as it did for Jesus.

The Gospel accounts now race through the nighttime ordeal of Jesus: hearings and trials in both the temple courts of Annas and Caiaphas and the civil courts of Pilate and Herod. As the story is told in the Gospel of John, the trials were taking place at two levels simultaneously. The trial of Jesus is mirrored in those who stand by and in those who sit in judgment upon Him. Let those who have eyes to see, see. In the religious courts, Peter is on trial during the hearings for Jesus. In the political courts, Pilate and Herod are on trial. In the whole ugly business, the chief priests of the temple and the scribes and Pharisees of Israel are on trial before the court of history.

We need to reflect on the story only briefly to realize that Peter, Pilate, and the priests are *us*. Jesus has tried since the retreat at Caesarea Philippi to prepare the disciples for His death. We wonder now if they are ready. Can they stand the test of the utterly devastating reality that is about to break upon them? What if they fail? Will they have a second chance? Will

Jesus be loyal to them should they fail? What of us? We are on trial as well.

During the first half of Jesus' ministry, His task is to help people see Him as the Christ—the mystery of messiahship. In the second half of the story, His task is to enable those who see Him as Messiah to penetrate the mystery of suffering and death. *Death* is the primary opponent for Jesus, for the disciples, for Pilate, for the religious leaders, and for us. Jesus faces death as the will of the Father in heaven. The disciples face death as the defeat of their freedom movement and the death of their dream of an ideal kingdom on earth under the control of Israel, God's chosen people. The rulers, both religious and political, see the death of Jesus as the solution to a political problem about the stability of their institutional structures. Jesus alone penetrates the mystery of death and discloses it to be the doorway into true freedom and life. He opens the door not in thought, however, but in behavior: in risking everything on the presence of God in death and beyond.

Observe the mirror images of the trial and sentencing of Jesus. Jesus is arrested and brought to Annas, the retired chief priest, for His first hearing. Immediately, Peter is spotlighted standing outside the door of the court of the high priest. Another disciple (presumably John), who has access to the court, "went out, spoke to the woman who guarded the door, and brought Peter in" (John 18:16). The woman then asks, "You are not also one of this man's disciples, are you?" Peter denies it. Jesus is then sent to Caiaphas's chambers. Caiaphas is the son-in-law of Annas and the reigning high priest. The dialogue between Peter and the people in the courtyard is given, and Peter denies being a disciple of Jesus a second time. Presumably, Jesus reenters the courtyard as He is taken from Caiaphas to Pilate's official residence, the Praetorium, so He possibly made eye contact with Peter just as Peter denies Him the third time—"and at that moment the cock crowed" as Jesus predicted (John 18:27). So who is found guilty at this stage? Not Jesus, but Peter, of course.

The action now shifts to the court of Pilate, the Roman governor. Pilate asks the question that is crucial for everyone meeting Jesus face-to-face: Who are you? Jesus defines Himself as a witness to the truth, and Pilate decides he is dealing with some kind of visionary over whom his court has no jurisdiction. So Pilate makes the first of several offers to release Jesus. The rulers of the temple ask for the release of Barabbas, a revolutionary being held for murder and for advocating the violent overthrow of Roman rule (John 18:38-40).

The scene is then repeated with Herod, who intensifies the action by authorizing ridicule and mocking (Luke 23:11) in response to Jesus' silence. So far, Jesus has not been found guilty of anything, but Pilate passes the buck, and Herod plays the bully.

So it is back to Pilate, where the buck finally stops. Pilate's overriding concern is to keep the peace in a highly volatile political climate. He tells Jesus' accusers that neither he nor Herod can find Jesus guilty of any of the charges against Him, but that he will "have him flogged and release him" (Luke 23:16). Pilate underestimates the fury of the priests. They confront him with a mass protest calling for the release of Barabbas. He tries twice more to work a compromise for the release of Jesus, "but they shouted out, 'Crucify, crucify him!' " (Luke 23:21).

Matthew's account adds two more details to the story. Pilate's wife sends him a message while he is in court, saying, "Have nothing to do with that innocent man, for today I have suffered a great deal because of a dream about him." Unwilling to risk a riot or to accept responsibility for sentencing an innocent man to death, Pilate then does his infamous hand washing, saying, "I am innocent of this man's blood; see to it yourselves" (Matt. 27:19-24).

John pronounces the guilty verdict against Pilate and the religious rulers in a final scene. The priests threaten Pilate, saying, "If you release this man, you are no friend of the emperor; everyone who claims to be a king sets himself against the emperor." Pilate then capitulates. He presents Jesus to His accusers, asking, "Shall I crucify your King?" The chief priests answer, "We have no king but the emperor."

Pilate's guilt cannot be washed away no matter how many ritual ablutions he may perform. He has sentenced an innocent man to crucifixion. The chief priests are guilty of an even more heinous crime. They have betrayed their God. In confessing Caesar to be their king, they declare a pagan emperor to be their Lord.

Jesus, then, is nailed to the cross, having been found innocent of the crimes with which He is charged. All those who participated in the hearings and the trial are guilty not only of the death of an innocent man but also of willing the death of God. Jesus is sovereign in His death. He bears His own cross. He dies voluntarily. In an act of supreme irony, Pilate identifies Jesus accurately by ordering the sign on His cross to read: "Jesus of Nazareth, the King of the Jews" (John 19:19).

Pilate has the answer to his first question: Who are You? He does not probe deeply enough to ask or answer the further questions: Where are You from? and "What is truth?" Jesus is not from Nazareth, but from God. The truth is a kingdom coming "On earth as it is in heaven." Had Pilate seen the truth about these questions, would he have capitulated under pressure of the priests and ordered Jesus' death?

A final question about the story begs to be asked. Does anyone in the story understand where Jesus is from or what His kingdom is about? Yes. The women understand. The nameless woman anointed Him for His death. At the foot of the cross, Mary, the mother of Jesus; Mary's sister, wife of Clopas and mother of James and Joses; Mary Magdalene; and Salome, the mother of the sons of Zebedee (James and John)—these were faithful to the end.

Were there no men? On Golgotha, only one disciple is identified: "the disciple whom he [Jesus] loved" (John 19:26); but the Roman soldiers who performed the executions exclaimed,

"Truly this man was God's Son!" (Matt. 27:54). We cannot forget Joseph of Arimathea and Nicodemus. Joseph has the courage to ask Pilate for Jesus' body and the generosity to provide a new tomb in which to bury Him. Nicodemus brings a hundred pounds of spices with which to prepare the body for burial. Joseph and Nicodemus not only identify themselves publicly as disciples, but they also make themselves ceremonially unclean in touching a dead body. During Passover Week, they dared violate social custom in doing what is strictly women's work in preparing the body for burial as well.

Some of these may understand who Jesus is as Son of God. Others are faithful without a clear theological vision. Some, like the Roman soldiers, may well confess Jesus to be a son of God in the sense that heroic patriots of Rome were declared to be "gods" after their death. Many are "little people" in the eyes of society; others are highly visible with prestigious positions; some are Jews, and others are Gentiles; some are women, and others are men. So today. Those who make the choice for discipleship do so out of many levels of insight, many backgrounds of ethnic origin, religion, sexual identity, nationality, political persuasion, age, and social position.

The Spirit of God is no respecter of persons in waking people to see who Jesus is, from whom He comes, and whose kingdom He opens to humankind. At the same time, the Spirit of God may be shut out by every variety of person. God is not impressed by human titles, degrees, or religious labels; nor is God intimidated by a person's power, intelligence, or level of spirituality. The door of the kingdom of God swings on tiny hinges. One must be willing to be as little children before the twin mysteries of who Jesus is and of the magnetic power of the cross to draw a person through death into true freedom and eternal life.

To amplify these two themes, we turn now to a story that helps us to look at the crucified Galilean through the eyes of Pilate, a Roman governor, and his wife, Claudia, who embodies the Greek and Egyptian influences in the patrician society of Rome.

Story: Claudia's Dream

Claudia drew a brush through her hair without delight in the image reflected in the mirrors before her. Absently, she fingered her white linen gown, reserved for the great festival of the passion and resurrection of Osiris. At the sound of her husband's boots reverberating against the marble floor outside her chambers, Claudia grasped the miniature statue of the goddess, Isis, and breathed a prayer for protection.

Blasting in and standing astride the doorway, Pontius Pilate bellowed: "You've had that priest of Isis here again, haven't you, Claudia? I spotted the white-robed vulture fleeing down the arcade as I returned!"

Claudia studied an age spot on the back of her hand.

"Look at you! You're wearing the festival gown. Why did you have him here? Speak up, woman! You know I have forbidden you to have that mongrel mystic in the Praetorium!"

Suddenly Claudia whirled off the bench, fought back an impulse to hurl the hairbrush at the accuser in her doorway, planted her feet under her, and screamed into his face, "You sentenced Him to death, didn't you! You had Him crucified! You have brought down the wrath of the gods upon our house. I warned you!"

She turned away and threw herself on to the bed, sobbing, "I tried to stop you, but you wouldn't listen to me. Now it's too late; it's too late."

"Yes, you warned me; and I'm warning you, woman. You violate the rules of the court again by sending in a report of your latest dream, and I'll ship you back to Caesarea where you can't interfere with matters of state." Pilate deflated his chest a bit, closed the door, and sat down as he began to undo his uniform and pull off his boots.

"You're being hysterical again, Dede." One of the children had coined Claudia's nickname years ago. "I only did what had to be done to keep the peace."

"It was horrible." Claudia drew up into a fetal position as she relived the dream that triggered this explosion of tempers.

"I dreamed that we are riding in state on the royal boat down a great, wide river. I speak of the beauty and fragrance of the flowering shrubs and trees growing on the banks. Our subjects cheer us joyfully. Suddenly, a fierce wind comes out of the west. The desert sands darken the sky. Our boat is driven aground. I cannot see or hear you. Terror pierces my heart. Then the wind dies down, and a blur of light appears. I think the sun is about to break through, but instead, it is the smirking face of Set, the evil god of the desert. I turn away, stumbling through the wreckage looking for you."

"Dede, Dede. That's enough. Forget the dream." But Claudia does not hear her husband's voice.

"I find you. Your body has been cut into fourteen bloody parts, laid out on the sand like meat in a butcher's shop. I scream, but my scream is swallowed up in the maniacal laughter of the evil god Set." Claudia's eyes are wide with horror, but she does not see Pontius bending over her. She sees only the horrible scene in her dream.

"I am putting the pieces of the body together again, but my tears blind me so that I cannot make them fit. I collapse in panic."

Pontius is shaking her now, "Dede! Dede! Come out of it! I'm here. It's OK. You're all right." But Claudia cannot be called back until her night horror has played itself out completely.

"Then my body warms. I think, *Apollo has come. The storm is over.* I lift my head and look up at the sun, only it is not the sun; it is the face . . . the face of that Galilean, Jesus. I know He has come for me. He is full of compassion, but I jump up and run . . . run . . . run . . ." Claudia is hyperventilating as she comes out of the spell and becomes aware of her husband holding her.

"So you called the priest to interpret your dream? What did he say, Dede? Tell me. It's better to know. Did the priest say he could make atonement for me?"

"The gods are angry with you, Pontius. The Galilean was innocent. He—the Galilean—came to take me away. The priest said that He came pretending to be Apollo, the light of truth, but wanting to rape me. He said it was good that I ran away."

"Dede, did he say he could make atonement for me?"

"Yes, of course. But you will have to pay dearly for it, you know." Claudia swallowed her thought: *and that priest's atonement will not be worth a denarius* [the daily wage of a laborer].

"Dede, I knew the Galilean was innocent of any crime deserving death. He was one of your simple mystics. He got Himself in trouble with the priests because He thought He was a god and was too out of touch with reality to keep His mouth shut."

"But He is a god, Pontius." Claudia trembled again with fear. "Death will not hold Him!"

"Not a god, Dede. A man. The only gods a Roman knows are the emperors: Julius Caesar was a god; Augustus was a god; and Tiberius . . ."

"No! No!" Claudia's anger was coming to her rescue now. "The gods become men, but men do not become gods! The gods rule our lives, Pontius. You governors and officers are mere puppets in their hands."

"If the gods are running things, why are we Romans ruling this god-crazy, fanatical little country of Israel? If the gods have anything to do with the real world, why are your Egyptian priests of Isis and Osiris taking orders from Rome? Be sensible, Dede! These other-worldly religions keep the masses pacified, but it's Roman organization and Roman energy and Roman power that rules the real world."

"Yes," Claudia whispered under her breath, "Rome has gained the whole world and lost her own soul."

"As for your Galilean, Dede," Pilate continued, "if a gentle, misguided mystic has to be sacrificed from time to time to keep the peace, so be it. At least Rome is keeping the peace for the whole civilized world."

"Well, if Caesar were a god," Claudia argued, "why did his wife, Calpurnia, try to keep him from going to the forum on the day of his death? Because she had been warned in a dream, that's why. Caesar had no use for the supernatural either, and you see where it got him. Today you, Pontius, have been just as big a fool!"

"A fool am I? Let me tell you what a fool would have done today. A fool sitting in my judgment seat would have set this Galilean free, and the fanatics would be in the streets this minute rioting. Then the fool would have emptied the barracks of Roman troops; blood would be flowing in the streets and in the temple. Most of all in the temple, for the chief priests are behind this whole dirty business. Then the fool would be shipping out to Rome to answer charges *again* for cruel and unnecessary use of force against the provincials."

Pilate was pacing the room now, lost in his oration, while Claudia rolled over on the bed exhausted.

"You know what Tiberius did to this fool the last time I called out the troops and sent them into the temple? He sided with the Sadducees who keep the tribute flowing to Rome and sent us back to this god-forsaken place of the empire—on probation.

"So, Dede, you just forget your bad dream; leave the priests and all their supernatural silliness to me. It wouldn't hurt you one bit to give me a little appreciation for what I've done today. I've run a tight ship. I had the good sense to ignore your hysterical message this morning. I negotiated my way out of a riot, and I proved to Rome that I can keep the peace in the hottest spot of the empire!

"Dede. Dede? She's gone to sleep on me. I'll call her maid to come and prepare her for bed. And I'll have a servant woman sent in to sit the night with her, just in case she has another nightmare."

Twenty-four hours later, after the Jewish Sabbath was over, the chief priests and the Pharisees came to the Praetorium to see Pilate. Claudia heard the servants laughing about the priests who were worrying lest the Galilean's disciples come to the tomb, steal Him away, and tell the people, "He has risen from the dead." They were proud of the way Pilate dismissed those pompous priests.

"You priests ought to get acquainted with Joseph of Arimathea," Pilate told them. "He buried your Galilean in a new tomb here that is fit for a king. If you Jerusalem priests had a speck of the decency of that man, you wouldn't have to worry about these country saints that steal the people's affections away from you. They might even like you for a change."

Later that same night, Claudia sat in her suite alone, writing a letter that she would send secretly and under cover of darkness to Joseph of Arimathea.

Joseph,
   Your tomb is empty now. Your Galilean is alive! He came to me last night and said: "I am risen! Let Osiris and Isis save Pilate if they can. I go ahead of my disciples to Galilee. I will see you there."
   Please, Joseph, send word by my messenger where I may find you in Galilee. I belong to your Galilean too.
                                                                         Sincerely,
                                                                         Claudia Procla
[Editor's note: History records that Claudia became a Christian and was later canonized by the Greek Orthodox Church.]

Comments on Story: Claudia's Dream

The Action

The action of the story takes place in Claudia's suite in the Roman governor's official residence in Jerusalem, known as the Praetorium. Outside the Praetorium, Jerusalem is crowded with pilgrims for the annual celebration of the Jewish Passover. As usual on high holy days, the Roman governor executes the latest political prisoners and common criminals. This year two inmates sit on death row, as it were. They are believed to be charged with sedition and are scheduled for crucifixion. On the night before the scheduled executions, the chief priests and rulers of the people bring a Galilean to Pilate insisting that He be crucified the next morning with the others. The priests have found Him guilty of heresy by claiming to be God, but the only charge that will qualify for crucifixion is sedition, advocating the violent overthrow of Roman rule. Crucifixion was the method of choice for such people. It was believed to inhibit revolutionary zeal against Rome because of the gross humiliation and indescribable physical torture it inflicted in its victims.

Inside the Praetorium, a domestic conflict flares between the governor and his wife, Claudia. The action amplifies a single verse in Matthew's account of the trial of Jesus before Pilate: "While he was sitting on the judgment seat, his wife sent word to him, 'Have nothing to do with that innocent man, for today I have suffered a great deal because of a dream about him'" (Matt. 27:19).

Night has fallen. Jesus is dead and buried. Pilate comes home feeling pleased with himself for having kept the peace and avoided another Passover riot. Knowing Claudia will be angry that he ignored her warning about the Galilean, he greets her with an outburst about her consorting with the Egyptian priests of Isis and Osiris. They exchange accusations about Pilate's behavior in court. Overpowered by her husband's high-handed treatment of her, Claudia flings herself on her bed and begins to relive the night horror that prompted her to violate court procedures and send a warning to Pilate while he presided on the judgment seat.

Next, the action goes inward. What is played out on the stage of Claudia's dream is the action that matters most. Her dream is a story within the story of her argument with her husband. We will attend to the dream story later in discussing themes.

Pilate has no interest in the symbolism of the dream at all. To him, Claudia is just a hysterical woman reacting to a nightmare. He got the message that she holds him guilty of the death of Jesus, however. His only concern is how to put her mind at ease about the matter so that she will not be a bother to him.

Therefore, Pilate makes sure the priest has agreed to make atonement for him and tries to end the matter by discounting Jesus as just a simple mystic who wasn't smart enough "to keep His mouth shut."

Claudia is no weakling who can be dismissed in such a patronizing way. She presses her case that Pilate has angered the gods and is in serious danger. She argues well, showing insight into the ways of the spirit world. The only world Pilate knows is the Roman world of empire, power, and heroic men who may earn the title of god as the supreme honor of the state. Their argument turns bitter as Claudia calls Pilate a fool. Pilate then swamps her with talk—defensive, self-justifying talk that reveals his anxiety about surviving as a quasi-military official of the empire and reveals that he is already on probation with Rome for his cruel and arbitrary use of force on the Jews a few years prior. Claudia escapes Pilate's self-defense by falling asleep, and the scene ends on a superficially solicitous tone.

The resolution of Claudia's inner conflict comes within the next twenty-four hours. Her servants give her the clue she needs. A Jewish man of integrity and equally high social status, Joseph of Arimathea, becomes the key to her escaping the consequences of Pilate's self-destructive act. Joseph also can open the door for Claudia to become a follower of the Galilean whose compassion has awakened her desire for God in a way nothing else has ever done before.

The message Claudia sent to Joseph of Arimathea tells us that even though Pilate ordered a servant to sit up with her in the night, he was unable to prevent the Galilean from appearing to her once again in a vision inviting her to join His disciples in Galilee.

Characters and Themes

The themes of the story are so interwoven in the character structure of Pilate and Claudia that they must be discussed together. Before attempting to do so, we turn to the story within the story: Claudia's dream.

Claudia dreams she is in Egypt, riding in state on the Nile River, with her husband at her side. Symbolically, she is Isis receiving the praise of her subjects with Osiris, her mythical husband, at her side. Suddenly, a violent wind storm strikes them with darkness and desert sands. Their boat runs aground. When Claudia finds her husband, his body has been cut into fourteen parts.

This part of the dream reenacts the ancient Egyptian myth in which Set, the brother and rival of Osiris, cuts him into fourteen pieces, and scatters his body parts around the world. Set is the god of the desert, an evil god, ambitious to gain control of Egypt and, therefore, constantly threatening Osiris and Isis.

Isis is the goddess of the fertile plains along the Nile, and Osiris is the god of the Nile who, in flooding the plains each year, fertilizes them and assures an abundant crop. In the myth, Isis persists in hunting for her husband's body, finally recovering all fourteen parts. She cunningly joins the fragments together and restores the murdered god to eternal life.

Osiris decides not to continue to live as a man on earth, however. Instead he becomes lord of the underworld and of the dead. The Egyptian underworld is on the bottom side of the earth and is the realm to which the sun retires during the night. Osiris is able thereby to guarantee eternal life to all who live well on earth and to transform the underworld from perpetual darkness to a realm blessed by the regular orbiting of the sun. Together, then, Isis protects the living and blesses them with grain and fruits in abundance while Osiris welcomes the deserving dead into a beatific realm below.

The Isis and Osiris myth offered political security to the ancient Egyptians as well. Their son, Horus, grew up to avenge his father's death against Set by defeating and restraining him (the evil power of the ever-threatening desert). Horus became identified with the Pharaohs and so assured the people that whenever an old Pharaoh died, a son and heir would arise to guarantee political stability for their nation.

Now, back to Claudia's dream. Claudia is terrorized by the

evil god of the desert and fails to put her husband's body back together again. Symbolically, for Claudia, her husband has lost his integrity in sentencing the Galilean to death. He has been overcome by evil, and she has lost her respect for him as well.

Jesus then appears in the final scene of her dream. Claudia experiences the Galilean as if He were Ra, the sun god—warm and compassionate. Frightened, nonetheless, she runs from Him and wakens in a panic.

What can we say, then, about these two embattled characters? What drove them apart? Why has the routine sentencing of another Jew charged with sedition triggered contempt for each other and been the occasion for Claudia to leave her husband, her religion, her good name, and a supposedly secure future as an honored Roman matron and the wife of a governor of the empire?

As the argument ends and Claudia falls asleep, nothing has been resolved in the conflict between them. One suspects that the marital conflict is chronic. Their differences run deep. Pilate has a legal mind; Claudia has a mystic's sensitivity to the unseen realm of the spirit. His world is concrete and sensate; hers is mythical and intuitive; he processes experience by thinking; she, by feeling; his is an ordered, predictable world; hers, a random world full of surprise. Pilate lives to please his emperor; Claudia, to please the gods.

Nothing has been resolved within Claudia either. Her priest has confirmed her fears that Pilate has angered the gods and will suffer (unless, of course, he pays dearly for a priestly atonement). She distrusts the priestly rituals, however. Her dream shows a truth far more profound than the priest cares to see. The desert has overcome the Nile. Her man has lost his integrity. He no longer will be potent as a man to beget life but only to destroy life and to spread decay and death in the world around him. Claudia now knows something else. She knows that she was warmed by the presence of the Galilean as by the sun. What does this mean for Claudia? Her priest attributes evil to the innocent Galilean, but Claudia knows better. Claudia knows it was the Galilean who overcame Set, the evil god of the desert. She felt His compassion awakening a desire so strong that it frightened her, causing her to run and run and run.

As the story ends, resolution has come at both levels: Claudia will leave Pilate for an unknown future. She has found acceptance, an inner peace and serenity beyond anything she has ever known, and a flaming devotion to the Galilean whom she now knows is a god, risen from the dead, with life-giving light of the sun in His eyes.

We know, too, that the resolution of the central conflicts in her life with Pilate will ignite a fire of conflict different than she has known before. Pilate and all her acquaintances will call her the fool: a Roman matron running after a band of Jewish revolutionaries . . . a governor's wife going counter-culture in a commune . . . a devotee of Isis, the great mother of the universe, giving her soul to the Spirit of a nobody crucified as a common criminal. "It's too bad about poor Claudia!" they will say. "Whatever possessed her to do such a stupid thing?"

Yet Claudia, like her Galilean, penetrated the mystery of the cross. She did so not in philosophy or in ritual, not by knowledge or by virtue. She did so in action, in life! She took up her cross and followed the Galilean. She became a fool in her desire for God. Today she lives in memory, canonized a saint by the Greek Orthodox Church.

7

To Life!

Every story starts out with a complication, moves through a series of conflicts, and ends with a resolution of some kind. The Jesus story is no exception. The initial complication is that God has decided to use ordinary people to bring His kingdom to earth as it is in heaven. God gets good enough cooperation at first to get Jesus born into a God-fearing family. Then comes conflict. The reigning king tries to kill the baby; and when the boy is grown and starts His mission, the ruling priests are so threatened that they plot to kill Him. Even His closest disciples misunderstand what kind of a kingdom they are supposed to be founding. When the agents of the Roman Empire collude with the priests to crucify Him, most of His disciples either betray, deny, or simply disappear, leaving Him to die in the company of the mocking crowds.

At first it appears there will be no resolution, unless utter failure is to be the theme. Then comes the resolution to the story. What a resolution it is! On the morning of the third day, Jesus rises from the dead. The tomb is empty. He appears to His dispirited followers, and sorrow turns to joy, doubt to faith, guilt to forgiveness, and despair to mission.

Through all the generations since, those who have chosen to become characters in the ongoing Jesus story have found resolution to the crises and conflicts in their days by discovering the inner meaning of the resurrection for their lives. The result has been amazing serenity in the face of martyrdom, energy in spite of discouragement, perseverance in the face of overwhelming opposition, fidelity in the face of temptation, and institutional renewal rising out of the foulest corruption.

What is this inner meaning of the resurrection? Is it faith in a final resolution of our conflicts in the hereafter? Must we wait on death to find the key to life? Or is there a reality in the stories of dying and rising again that is available here and now? What does the central story of the Christian Scriptures say to us about life today? What is the goal of the Christian adventure?

To address these questions, we tell another story. It happened at the most critical moment in the postresurrection story of the Jesus movement. It happened in Jerusalem about A.D. 55, approximately twenty-five years after Jesus' death and resurrection.

Story: Do Not Hold Me!

I was so excited that day as we made ready to receive the apostle Paul. Our whole community, the Poor Ones of Jerusalem, was in a flurry preparing for the reception. We were honoring Paul in behalf of the whole Jerusalem church, saying "thank you" for the offering he had brought from the Gentile churches. Paul had asked for some private time with Mary of Magdala after the reception, for at that time Mary had been bedfast for several months.

Mary had chosen me to attend her in what proved to be her final illness. I suppose that is why the sisters were determined that I should write the story of her meeting with Paul and with James, the brother of Jesus and ruling elder of the Jerusalem church. It all happened during two fateful weeks after Paul's arrival.

"The sisters are saying that the gift will sustain our house forever if it is managed well." I could hardly contain myself as I shared the news. "Oh, Mary, isn't God good to let you live to see this wonderful day!"

"Yes, Judith," Mary replied. "Most of all, I praise Rabboni for the hope Paul brings with his gift—for the breaking down of the wall between Jews and Gentiles of 'The Way.' "

"Just let me fluff your pillows, Mary, and you will be all ready to receive the apostle." As Paul entered the room, I took a seat in the corner.

"Mary, how I have longed for an opportunity to meet you." Paul was not an imposing man to look at, but his spirit was contagious from his first word. "You were the first and I the last to see the risen Christ. You have embodied His Spirit here in Jerusalem, and I have tried to be true to my calling among the Gentiles."

"Yes, Paul, we know the mystery of being one 'in Christ.' " A beautiful and pregnant silence filled the room. The Spirit of God was felt. "You have risked your life to come to Jerusalem at this time, Paul. We are all aware of the vision given to Agabus warning you not to come, but we are so grateful . . ." Mary's voice choked with the feelings she was fighting back.

"Neither of us knows how much time we have left here, Mary. For a long while now, I have known that for me to live is Christ and to die is gain."

Becoming more intense, Paul continued, "Nothing is more important to the kingdom now than for us to preserve the unity of the church. I simply cannot stand back and see this sectarian hysteria tear us apart. In Christ there is no such thing as Jew or Gentile, slave or free, male or female."

"I cannot tell you, Paul, how distressing it is to me to see the Jerusalem church being swept away by the Zealot's fantasy that Rabboni will return with legions of angels to make Jerusalem the capital of the world. An evil spirit is spreading darkness over us, as on the day of His crucifixion."

"I have been told, Mary, that since Peter left on his mission to the Jews of the dispersion, James has taken the church back to Jewish messianism, that the kingdom of God has become a political dream once again . . ."

"The very trap that Rabboni tried so hard to deliver us from when He was with us! But, of course, James was not one of us then."

"We both were in training for the priesthood then, Mary.

You know how threatened I was by Jesus and you people who were following Him." Paul flushed with shame in remembering his career as a Pharisee inquisitor.

"Yes, Paul, I know." Mary spoke with deep sadness and without bitterness. "I fear that James may do more to destroy Rabboni's truth as His disciple than you did as our persecutor."

"Mary, the hardest truth I had to confront, after facing up to my own corrupt heart, was my pride in being among the elect, the chosen people of God. Now that I see the Christ as the Savior of the whole world, and not an exclusively Jewish Messiah, I know that the gospel I preach is 'bad news' for every zealous patriot among us. Believe me, Mary, I understand how hard it must be for James and the whole church of Jerusalem to question being the elect of God."

"You underestimate the problem, Paul. It's so much worse than a theological question. Were any of us to say what you have just said about Jesus as Messiah for the Gentiles as well as for us, we would be marked for the Zealot 'death squads.' James and the others know this all too well."

"So, it has come to this." Paul became pensive. The silence was frightening. "I see it now," Paul said, "James is nailed to the cross already. If he remains true to his agreement that we take the gospel to the Gentiles, he risks death not only for himself but also for the mother church here in Jerusalem."

"Oh, Paul." Mary reached out for Paul to hold her hand. Tears filled her eyes. "If only I could help James to see what I came to see so many years ago, as I stood weeping outside the tomb. I saw a man standing there, saying 'Woman, why are you weeping? Whom do you seek?' I thought He was the gardener. Then He called my name, and I knew Him, my Rabboni!

"I have relived that moment a thousand times." Mary was so alive as she remembered. "In these desperate days I see how easy it is to mistake the gardeners of the church for our risen Lord. All of us who spend our lives tending the institutions of our faith—we are just the gardeners. Beyond the gardeners stands Rabboni, calling us by name, calming our fears, and assuring us that He is risen. His kingdom will come—not because of the gardeners but by His Spirit alive in the world." Mary fell back on her pillows, her energy spent. Instinctively, I stood up to go to her. Paul stood too. We both knew that the visit was over.

"Thank you, Mary, for an image I shall never forget: seeing the difference between the gardeners and our risen Lord." He pronounced a blessing on Mary and on our whole house, and then he left. I think we all knew that we were never to meet each other again—until the resurrection.

For days Mary scarcely ate or spoke. I did not tell her about James's plan for reassuring the militant faction at church. He prevailed on Paul to sponsor four young men who were taking their final vows as Nazirites. So at considerable expense to himself, Paul spent the next seven days in the temple, making sacrifice for the initiates, and observing the rites of purification.

But the Zealots were not to be denied their victim. As Paul completed his vigil with the Nazirites, on the seventh day they started a riot with false rumors that Paul had taken his Gentile friend, Trophimus the Ephesian, into the court of the Israelites with him. The whole city went mad with rage. Supposing Paul had violated temple law, they dragged him into the court of the Gentiles. They were starting to beat him to death as the Roman soldiers, coming through the secret passageway, arrived to restore order.

Paul was subjected to the inquisition of the council most of the next day. On the following morning, as we learned later, a group of more than forty Zealots bound themselves by an oath neither to eat nor drink until they had killed Paul. They went to the chief priests and elders of the council and conspired with them to request the Roman officers to bring Paul to them the next day as though they were going to determine his case more exactly. The Zealot band planned to kill him en route from the prison to the meeting with the council.

Providence intervened. Paul had been staying with his sister and her family who have lived in Jerusalem for years. Their ten-year-old boy, Eli, was stretched out behind the balustrade, near the Gate of the Flame. He was waiting for his mother who was inside (in the court of the women) praying for her brother at that very moment. Eli's attention was caught by two men slipping around the back corner of the temple. He lay flat against the balustrade, and the men stopped almost at the very spot where Eli was, but with their backs to him. He heard every word. One of them was telling the other, "The council has just agreed to call Paul back for another hearing." He told the man just where they were to meet to set their ambush.

In no time, Eli's mother prepared a cake and some fruit and sent Eli to take them to his uncle. She knew that a centurion who was a member of our church was on duty that day, and he would let Eli deliver the food in person. It would have been against the rules to let an adult relative in, you see. But no one would suspect the boy.

Paul had the guard take little Eli to the tribune, who took him aside and asked him privately what he had to say. The tribune then sent the boy home warning him to tell no one that Eli had informed the tribune of the assassination plot.

That night, a party of two hundred soldiers with seventy horsemen and two hundred spearmen escorted Paul to Caesarea, into the charge of Felix the governor.

You can imagine what a celebration we had here when word came back that Paul was safe in Caesarea. I could no longer keep the news from Mary, of course. In fact, she sensed that something unusual was going on and insisted that I tell her everything.

The next day, Mary sent me on the most frightening errand of my years as a novitiate among the Poor Ones of Jerusalem. I felt that I would suffocate as I made my way through the crowds to the headquarters of the mother church. "If only I did not have to wear this veil," I kept saying to myself, "I would not feel so faint."

Looking back, though, I know it was not the veil on my face

but the fear around my heart. Somehow I must have known that our revered Mary of Magdala was dying. I could never have forced myself out onto the streets nor on to my meeting with our ruling elder, James, had I not felt compelled by an overriding urgency.

I waited for hours outside the elder's office while men were ushered in to do their business with him. There were elders and brothers, a committee of Pharisees, Galilean and Judean priests doing duty at the temple, and two of the most dangerous Zealots in Jerusalem.

The assistant began to close up for the day before he spoke to me again: "Sorry, woman, we're closing for the day. Perhaps you could come back tomorrow." Somehow, beyond my knowing, I stood up and blocked the outside doorway, just as the elder came out of his office. I opened my mouth to speak, but not a sound came out. My arm shot out, however, shaking the note from Mary in front of his eyes.

"And how is our beloved lady," James asked me as he folded up the note.

"Very weak," I whispered. "It's urgent, sir."

"I'll come with you now, Sister . . ."

"Judith," I said, knowing he would not remember and wondering why I bothered to give him my name.

Mary seemed stronger than she had been in weeks when I ushered the ruling elder into her presence. Her eyes had their old intensity. Her voice was deep and firm.

"James, how good of you to come," she said, extending her hand.

"It is always a benediction for me to be in your presence, dear lady. As I have told you so many times, being in the presence of the lady to whom my brother first appeared after His resurrection brings me so much closer to Him again."

"May God grant it to be so today," Mary replied.

"Our honored prophetess has a word for me, perhaps?" I could tell that James was bracing himself for an uncomfortable time.

"I am told that the apostle Paul escaped the Zealots' assassination plot and is now safe under Roman guard in Caesarea."

"You have heard correctly. God used his nephew to bring Paul word of the plot."

"I also understand," Mary continued, not allowing their meeting to turn into a news report, "that the elders of the church have decided to avoid a confrontation with the Zealots who fomented this evil business."

"To defend Paul in the present climate, Mary, would put us on the side of the Sadducean sacerdotal aristocracy. There is no middle position anymore."

I could not help admiring James for the way he came straight to the point. I realized, too, that he was taking our Mary of Magdala seriously.

"So by our silence, the Jerusalem church condones violence as a means to bring in the kingdom of peace."

"By our caution we protect the mother church, Mary. By the providence of God, Paul is safe in the hands of the Roman judicial system now. We must concentrate on keeping the temple out of captivity to the high priest and his Sadducean collaborators with Rome."

"James, have you forgotten the word of the Master, 'he who takes up the sword will perish by the sword'? Do we not put the church in greater jeopardy by colluding with assassins than by renouncing them?"

"My brother also said He had come not to destroy the law but to fulfill it. Granted it was a case of mistaken identity that set the whole ruckus in motion, but the law requires that one who profanes the temple by bringing a Gentile through the Nicanor Gate is to be put to death." James was beginning to sound like the scribes, but Mary would have none of it.

"James, our brother is the Lord. The risen Lord appeared to Saul on the Damascus Road and commissioned him to take the gospel to the Gentiles. All Jerusalem admires your devotion to the temple, James, but our gospel is not a gospel of the temple but of a kingdom of love for *all* people—Jew and Gentile alike."

"Times have changed, Mary. The 'glory days' when our Messiah walked the roads of Palestine, healed the sick, and cast out demons—yes, when He cleansed your soul, Mary—those days are gone.

"A universal kingdom? Paul's vision of Jew and Gentile at peace with one another 'in Christ'? A dream for another day, another time, perhaps. Today our only hope is in fidelity to the temple. We Christians are 'the salt of the earth,' 'the light of the world.' We must set the standard for a holy nation. We who are priests must be a royal priesthood. All of us must be 'the people prepared'—prepared for the return of the Christ with His legions of angels. He then will restore the kingdom to Israel. That will be the time to reach out to the Gentiles. It is for this we must pray, Mary. Only in the messianic kingdom will it ever be 'on earth as it is in heaven.' "

As the elder lectured, I saw the light go out of Mary's eyes. She lay back on her bed for what seemed an eternity. James reached out and took her hand and was silent. I realized for the first time that James had won the hearts of our church by his unusual combination of passion for Israel, which made him sound like a Zealot revolutionary, and compassion for individuals such as I was seeing now, as he held the hand of Mary of Magdala.

James pronounced his priestly blessing and took his leave.

As he left, Mary spoke into the empty space between them, "Rabboni, your Spirit has departed from Jerusalem. They are trying to bury mother church in the tomb of ambition for an imperial kingdom. Forgive them, for they know not what they do!"

I could not hold back my tears. Mary became aware of me then and reached for my hand. I fell on her and held her with both arms, clinging to her and sobbing, "Mary, Mary. Don't leave us! We need you. We need you!"

She opened her eyes one last time, with an arm across my shoulder, and said, "Fear not, my child. God will empty this tomb also. The Spirit of Jesus will be released to the whole world. Nothing, not even Rome, can prevent Him."

"And, Judith. Dear, dear Judith." Mary's voice was fading out. I laid my ear at her mouth, afraid to breathe. "I once held Him as you are holding me. He said, 'Do not hold on to me, . . . I am ascending to my Father and your Father' [John 20:17]. Now it is my time. I go—to life! So, Judith, do not hold on to me!"

In Retrospect

Within seven years of the death of Mary of Magdala, James, the brother of Jesus, ruling elder of the Jerusalem church, was stoned to death by order of the Sanhedrin. He was victim of an effort by the high priest to pacify the revolutionary fervor of the lower level priests, the Pharisees, and the Zealots, many of whom were members of the Jerusalem church. We sisters of the Poor Ones knew it was Mary's caution and her dying prayer that turned James to a more Christlike position and so led to his death at the hands of the extremists. I often wish that Mary could have lived to see the answer to her prayer for James. She would have been so grateful to her "Rabboni" and so proud of James for surrendering fully to Jesus—not as his older brother, but as his Lord.

Four years later, Titus, the emperor of Rome, launched what they called "the final solution for the Jewish problem." After a devastating four-year war [A.D. 70], Jerusalem was destroyed. The temple and the entire structure of our Jewish state was wiped off the face of the earth. Only a remnant of the mother church survived by fleeing to Pella across the Jordan River.

Paul won his appeal to Rome, and as a prisoner, continued to write letters to the churches of the Gentile world. He succeeded in freeing "the Jesus Way" from the legalism of the extremists among us [the Judaizers] on the one hand and the excesses of the mystery religions of the empire on the other.

Mary's hope was vindicated. In these tragic events, the tomb of the Jerusalem church was opened, and the Spirit of Christ was resurrected again—with good news for the poor, release to the captives, recovering of sight to the blind, setting at liberty the oppressed, and proclaiming "the year of the Lord's favor" (Luke 4:18-19).

And I? I was one of the few who escaped the carnage of the war. We now live in Alexandria, the Poor Ones of Egypt. Never did we know such poverty in Jerusalem, but we are living where our Lord also found asylum as a child. Never have we felt closer to Him. We have been cleansed at last of our pride of race. We have learned what Mary knew about the difference between the gardeners of the church and the risen Lord. At times I feel as if God's kingdom almost has come "On earth as it is in heaven."

Comments on Story: Do Not Hold Me!

The Conflict

The story is set in Jerusalem about twenty-five years after the crucifixion and resurrection of Jesus. The two-week period of the story well may have been the most critical turning point in the history of Christianity.

First, we need to understand the makeup of the Jerusalem church in its first-quarter century. After Pentecost, the followers of Jesus in Jerusalem created a close-knit community. There is evidence that the women known as the Poor Ones of Jerusalem (whom we met first in ch. 2 in relation to Simeon and Anna) provided a nucleus for the Jerusalem church. It mushroomed by the thousands in the early years, however. By the time of our story, the mother church was made up of the people of the land who were strongly opposed to the pro-Roman priestly aristocracy that was centered in the temple. Their membership included many lower-level priests who came from the rural areas to do temple duty periodically. Many Pharisees joined the Jerusalem church as did Zealots who were the outlawed "freedom fighters" of the Jews committed to achieve independence from Rome.

Looking back across a canyon of two thousand years, we find

it hard to believe that representatives of the very groups who conspired to kill Jesus were active in the Jerusalem church so soon after His death. Even more startling is the strong faction trying to transform Jesus' kingdom of love into a militant, fanatically patriotic conquest, establishing a world empire in which Jerusalem would displace Rome and the resurrected Jesus would reign forever.

The end of such a kingdom of God on earth justifies any means. For the Zealots, this meant readiness to assassinate those who dissented from their cause. Whether there were Christians among the Zealots who vowed to assassinate Paul, we cannot know. However, Zealot ideals and aggressiveness were clearly evident in the biblical record of the opposition of the "Judaizers" who went out from the Jerusalem church to undo the work of Paul in new churches throughout the Roman Empire.

Zealotism was a "noble expression of Jewish religious faith." It was "sanctioned and inspired by the example of many revered figures of Israel's heroic past."[1] Israel enjoyed political independence for almost one hundred and fifty years (approximately 170-129 B.C.). Prior to the events in the story, however, first Greece and then Rome had ruled the land for almost two hundred years. The process of Hellenization (acquiring Greek culture) had been going on for many generations, therefore, resulting in many compromises between the Jewish way of life and the prevailing culture of the Mediterranean world.

The platform of the Zealots, with strong support from the Pharisees and most of the lower level priests, was the Torah; an autocratic, hierarchical priesthood, centered in the temple in Jerusalem; and a God-centered culture rigidly bound by the traditional laws and customs of the centuries. Parallels with contemporary movements in both the Moslem and Christian faiths are obvious.

Over against some members of the mother church stood Paul and the new Christians, both Gentiles and Jews, throughout the Roman Empire. In particular, it was the church of Antioch that initiated the first showdown with the the Jerusalem church. To understand the conflict that comes to a head in the story, we must look at a theological difference between Paul and the Judaizers.

Paul had made sense out of his dramatic conversion by centering on the crucifixion of Jesus and the cross as the key to the Christian way of life. The Judaizers in the Jerusalem church had accepted the Suffering Servant prophecies about the Messiah in order to make sense out of Jesus' crucifixion, but they did not have the same understanding of the cross as the central metaphor for following in "the Way."

For Paul, the cross meant turning away from the Jewish concept of salvation as the redemption of Israel from heathen oppression. It meant that humankind as a whole was in a state of perdition through its subjection to the demonic powers that ruled the universe. Salvation was the rescue of all people, Jews and Gentiles, from bondage to sin and evil. This offer of universal salvation was made possible by Jesus' death, according to a divine plan, in order to overcome the power of evil once for all.[2]

Paul accused his critics from the Jerusalem church of imposing their ancient laws, such as circumcision, on the Gentile converts "only that they may not be persecuted for the cross of Christ" (Gal. 6:12). The danger to Jerusalem Christians was real. For to see the cross as God's way of opening salvation to the whole world meant that they would be in real danger of persecution by their Zealot neighbors. The leaders of the church would have been marked for assassination by the Zealot "death squads."

For the Judaizers, the cross meant a way of life dedicated to mobilizing a revolutionary movement of people prepared to die "with Christ" in the freedom fight against Rome. The final battle would prepare the way for Christ to return with legions of angels. The capital city for the kingdom of God on earth would be Jerusalem, of course, and the officials of the kingdom would be the zealous and legally pure sons of the covenant. Though there were differences between the Christian Judaizers and the non-Christian Zealots, the Jesus movement and the Zealot movement may have converged in the end on revolutionary military action in Jerusalem.[3]

You may wonder how a split this deep could have divided the early Christians, since the Book of Acts records a conference in Jerusalem some years prior to our story that negotiated an agreement between the two factions.

Peter led the Jerusalem church to become open to the conversion of Gentiles. His vision at the house of Cornelius, a Roman centurion, was for Peter as dramatic a conversion as was Paul's encounter with the risen Christ on the Damascus Road (see Acts 10:1—11:18). Returning to the Jerusalem church, Peter was required to give account for having violated Jewish law in eating with Gentiles. Peter's critics were silenced after hearing the story of what amounted to a Gentile Pentecost. "And they praised God, saying, 'Then God has given even to the Gentiles the repentance that leads to life' " (Acts 11:18).

This was not the beginning of an all-out mission to the Gentiles, however. Paul and Barnabas began their missionary work, but a faction within the Jerusalem church became more and more aggressive in sending their own missionaries to follow Paul and Barnabas with the requirement that new Christians honor the Torah by keeping the laws in every detail. The central point of dispute was the requirement of circumcision for males.

Dissension soon reached a fever pitch. The Judaizers insisted, "Unless you are circumcised according to the custom of Moses, you cannot be saved" (Acts 15:1). So the church in Antioch initiated a conference with the Jerusalem church to iron out their differences. After intense debate, Peter tipped the balance in favor of a compromise to which all parties agreed. Representatives of the Jerusalem church traveled to Antioch with Paul and Barnabas and reported the agreement in these words: "It has seemed good to the Holy Spirit and to us to impose on you no further burden than these essentials: that you abstain from what has been sacrificed to idols and from blood and from what is strangled and from fornication. If you keep yourselves from these, you will do well" (Acts 15:28-29).

By the time Paul brings the offering from the Gentile churches, James, the brother of Jesus, has become head of the Jerusalem church. Peter no longer appears. It is believed that he has been active for some time evangelizing among the synagogues in Egypt and other regions to which Paul and Barnabas have not gone. So the climate of the Jerusalem church has changed since the days of the previous conference. The temple is militantly anti-Gentile, and the Zealots are able to do as they please, with the collusion of the official council.

Paul was not willing to write off the Judaizers who were harassing him and his new converts. He was not willing to cut off himself or his churches from their heritage in Judaism or from their mother church in Jerusalem. It was his passion for unity in a church inclusive of Gentiles and Jews alike that inspired him to promote an offering from the Gentile churches to the poor of Jerusalem.

When he had come to Caesarea en route to Jerusalem to deliver the offering, a prophet named Agabus came down from Judea to warn Paul that he would be imprisoned if he insisted on going to Jerusalem at that time. It was this same devotion to the cause of unity that compelled him to say to those who begged him not to go, "What are you doing, weeping and breaking my heart? For I am ready not only to be bound but even to die in Jerusalem for the name of the Lord Jesus" (Acts 21:13).

The Action of the Story

Against this background and in the passionate tensions of the day, Paul and James meet. The action is viewed from the bedside of Mary of Magdala and told by Judith, a novitiate in the community of the Poor Ones of Jerusalem.

On the stage of the story, the action is limited to two conversations: the meeting between Mary and Paul, and between Mary and James. From the wings of the stage, we hear the noise of conflict between the rival factions of the church: James's

160 THE CHRISTIAN ADVENTURE

strategy to make Paul "clean" in the eyes of the zealous members of the mother church, the riot at the temple in which Paul was nearly killed, the whispers of the assassins, and the hoofbeats of the Roman soldiers as they escort Paul by night out of the Jerusalem caldron into the Roman judicial system in Caesarea.

The Characters and Themes

Mary is the central character of the story. Both Paul and James are important mainly as representatives of the forces that are moving on collision course within the mother church.

Mary is the same person who appears in the Gospels under the name of Mary Magdalene, out of whom Jesus cast seven demons. She was reared in the town of Magdala, on the west side of the Sea of Galilee. She was likely about the same age as Jesus but from a well-to-do family. She is mentioned as one of the women who traveled with the disciples and supported them financially. The reference to seven demons tells us that she was severely crippled by multiple problems. In the Gospel accounts demon-possessed persons were always portrayed as individuals in spiritual, physical, emotional and/or moral bondage. All we can be sure about is that Mary of Magdala was delivered by Jesus from multiple and extremely serious and oppressive difficulties. She was among the faithful few at the cross and was the first person to whom Jesus appeared after His resurrection.

In the story, Mary has remained in Jerusalem after the resurrection and become the great mother of the community of the Poor Ones of Jerusalem. She is now bedridden and facing her final hour. Through her eyes, as a saint of the church who understood the true nature of the kingdom Jesus meant to bring to the world, we see that it is not only Mary of Magdala who faces death at the end of a long life. It is also the mother church in Jerusalem that faces extinction along with the fanatics who are inflamed with a lust for power, veiled under their zeal for God.

In identifying with Mary, we experience the central conflict and theme of the story. The conflict is hope versus despair in the face of the death of all that one holds dear. Far more alarming to Mary of Magdala than her own imminent death is the captivity of the mother church to forces of militancy, lust for power, and the attending cruelties, deceptions, compromises, and contempt for life. Worst of all, for Mary, is the betrayal of her Rabboni's gospel of the kingdom of God—a kingdom "not of this world," as Jesus told Pilate. The kingdom is known by its inclusiveness rather than exclusiveness, by humility not pride, and by suffering in the service of love rather than of conquest.

Mary has faced this crisis before. A quarter of a century ago, she stood in a garden outside a tomb early on Sunday morning. She mourned the death of all her hopes for the healing of a world that drove people like her into absolute captivity to demonic powers. Inside that tomb lay the One who brought health and salvation to her. Inside that tomb lay the One who gave sight to the blind and life to the dead; who embraced lepers and little children; who valued women as persons in their own right rather than as property to be controlled and exploited. Buried were her hopes for a temple cleansed of its delusions of superiority and freed from its exploitation of the people who came to it in their desire for God.

Then Mary made a profound discovery. The gardeners at the tombs where one's hopes lie buried are not the same as the risen Christ. Mary learned at the empty tomb that the destiny of God's will for the world is in God's hands, not in human hands. God who was "Abba" to Jesus is Almighty in human history. This was a lesson she could never forget. So, now, as the Jerusalem church is being tempted to choose a grandiose fantasy that leads to death, Mary can say, "God will open this tomb also. The Spirit of Jesus will be released to the whole world. Nothing, not even Rome, can prevent Him."

Again, in the closing moments of her life, Mary Magdala sees an empty tomb beyond the tragic destruction of Jerusalem and the mother church. She hears the voice of Jesus, echoing through the years, saying, "Do not hold on to me."

She passes the vision of the Christian adventure on to her

faithful attendant and friend, Judith. And also to us. "Do not hold on to anything your heart holds dear," she is saying. In letting go, you are free to claim life in the here and now; to claim life in eternity; to give life to your children, to your race, your nation, and your world; and to affirm life for the Jesus story as it continues to be lived generation after generation.

Notes

1. S. G. Brandon, *Jesus and the Zealots: A Study of the Political Factor in Primitive Christianity* (New York: Charles Scribner's Sons, 1967), 63-64.

2. Gunther Bornkamm, *Paul*, trans. M. G. Stalker (New York: Harper & Row, Publishers, 1971).

3. Brandon, *Jesus and the Zealots*, 356.

Bibliography

INTRODUCTIONS TO THE GOSPELS AS STORY

Culpepper, R. Alan. *Anatomy of the Fourth Gospel: A Study in Literary Design.* Philadelphia: Fortress Press, 1983.

Edwards, O. C. Jr. *Luke's Story of Jesus.* Philadelphia: Fortress Press, 1981.

Kingsbury, Jack Dean. *Matthew as Story.* Philadelphia: Fortress Press, 1986.

Kysar, Robert. *John's Story of Jesus.* Philadelphia: Fortress Press, 1984.

Rhoads, David, and Donald Michie. *Mark as Story: An Introduction to the Narrative of a Gospel.* Philadelphia: Fortress Press, 1982.

COMMENTARIES AND BIBLE DICTIONARIES MOST CONSISTENTLY USED

Albright, William F., and David N. Freedman. *The Anchor Bible.* 51 vols. New York: Doubleday and Company, Inc., 1964-.

Buttrick, George A. *The Interpreter's Bible.* 12 vols. Nashville: Abingdon Press, 1951-57.

_____. *The Interpreter's Dictionary of the Bible: An Illustrated Encyclopedia.* Nashville: Abingdon Press, 1962-76.

Davis, John D., ed. *The Westminster Dictionary of the Bible.* Revision and rewrite by Henry S. Gehman. Philadelphia: The Westminster Press, 1944.

Mays, James L., Patrick D. Miller, Jr., and Paul J. Achtemeier, eds. *Interpretation: A Bible Commentary for Teaching and Preaching Series.* Atlanta: John Knox Press, 1982-91.

SOURCES ON DAILY LIFE IN THE TIME OF JESUS

Daniel-Pops, Henri. *Daily Life in the Time of Jesus.* Translated by Patrick O'Brian. Ann Arbor: Servant Books, 1980.

Jeremias, Joachim. *Jerusalem in the Time of Jesus.* London: SCM Press, Ltd., 1969.

The Mishnah. Translated by Herbert Danby. Oxford University Press, 1933.

Stagg, Evelyn, and Frank Stagg. *Woman in the World of Jesus.* Philadelphia: The Westminster Press, 1978.

SOURCES ON POLITICAL MOVEMENTS IN JESUS' DAY

Bammel, Ernst, and C. F. D. Moule, eds. *Jesus and the Politics of His Day.* New York: Cambridge University Press, 1984.

Brandon, S. G. *Jesus and the Zealots: A Study of the Political Factor in Primitive Christianity.* New York: Charles Scribner's Sons, 1967).

Cullmann, Oscar. *Jesus and the Revolutionaries.* New York: Harper & Row, Publishers, 1970.

Forster, Werner. *Palestinian Judaism in New Testament Times.* London: Oliver and Boyd, 1964.

Horsley, Richard. *Jesus and the Spiral of Violence: Popular Jewish Resistance in Roman Palestine.* San Francisco: Harper & Row, 1987.

Horsley, Richard, and John Hanson. *Bandits, Prophets, and Messiahs.* New York: Winston Press, 1985.

Safrai, S., and M. Stern, eds. *The Jewish People in the First Century.* 2 vols. Philadelphia: Fortress Press, 1974.

SOURCES ON THE RELIGIONS OF THE GREEK AND ROMAN WORLDS

Angus, S. *The Mystery-Religions: A Study of the Religious*

Background of Early Christianity. New York: Dover Publications, Inc., 1925, 1975.

Grant, Michael. *Roman Myths*. New York: Charles Scribner's Sons, 1971.

Meyer, Marvin W. ed. *The Ancient Mysteries: A Sourcebook*. Harper & Row, Publishers, 1987.

Solmsen, Friedrich. *Isis Among the Greeks and Romans*. London: Harvard University Press, 1979.

SOURCES ON WRITING FICTION

Cassill, R. V. *Writing Fiction*. New York: Prentice Hall Press, 1975.

Franklin, Jon. *Writing Fiction*. a Mentor Book (New American Library, 1986).

SOURCES CITED

Bonhoeffer, Dietrich. *The Cost of Discipleship*. New York: Macmillan, 1963.

Bornkamm, Gunther. *Paul*. Translated by M. G. Stalker. New York: Harper & Row, Publishers, 1971.

Brandon, S. G. *Jesus and the Zealots: A Study of the Political Factor in Primitive Christianity*. New York: Charles Scribner's Sons, 1967.

Brown, Raymond E. *The Birth of the Messiah: A Commentary on the Infancy Narratives in Matthew and Luke*. Garden City, N.Y.: Doubleday & Company, Inc., 1977.

_____. *New Testament Essays*. New York: Paulist Press, 1965.

The Epic of Gilgamesh. Introduced by N. K. Sandars. New York: Penguin Books, 1960.

Gelin, Albert. *The Poor of Yahweh*. Translated by K. Sullivan. Collegeville, Minn.: Liturgical Press, 1964.

Hengel, Martin. *Crucifixion in the Ancient World and the Folly of the Message of the Cross*. Philadelphia: Fortress Press, 1977.

Parrot, Andre. *The Temple of Jerusalem*. London: SCM, 1957.

Stauffer, Ethelbert. *Jesus and the Wilderness Community at Qumran.* Biblical Series, translated by Hans Spaltehaly, no. 10. Philadelphia: Fortress Press, Facet Books, 1964.